Mike

Many thanks for all your efforts on the tour committee

PANORAMIC
New Zealand

PANORAMIC

NEW ZEALAND

PHOTOGRAPHS BY TIM SNOWDON   TEXT BY SUSAN SNOWDON

HarperCollins*Publishers New Zealand Limited*

First published 1996
HarperCollins*Publishers (New Zealand) Limited*
P.O. Box 1, Auckland

Copyright © Tim Snowdon, Susan Snowdon

All rights reserved. No part of this publication
may be reproduced, stored in a retrieval system or transmitted
in any form or by any means, electronic, mechanical, photocopying,
recording or otherwise, without the prior written permission
of the publishers.

ISBN 1 86950 202 7

Designed by Pages Literary Pursuits
Printed by HarperCollins, Hong Kong

I dedicate this book to my wife Sue.
'You have stolen my heart with one glance of your eyes.'
Song of Songs

ACKNOWLEDGEMENTS

This project would never have been finished without the help of so many people: flying us in helicopters, letting us catch the dawn in a vineyard, stopping trains, chasing whales, guiding us on volcanoes or up mountains, taking us on jet boats, suspending us over bungy jumpers, halting the harvesting, or even letting me clamber over their roof to get the best vantage point. To all our friends who helped us complete this book, thank you so much for the cheerful support you showed to Sue and me, without you we would never have finished. I used Fuji Provia 100 film for most of the photographs, except in dull conditions in which case Fuji Velvia was used.

I would like to acknowledge the support of the following companies: Agrodome; Whakarewarewa Thermal Reserve; Waitomo Caves; Mission Vineyard; The Grand Chateau; Restaurant 360°; Orakei Korako; Michael Fowler Centre; The New Zealand International Festival of the Arts; Awaroa Lodge; Tasman Bay Aviation; Creeksyde Campervan Park; Whale Watch™; Shantytown; Lyttelton Timeball Station; Olveston; Lanarch Castle; Taieri Gorge Railway Ltd; Mount Cook Airline; Rippon Vineyard; Shotover Jetboats; Skippers Canyon Jetboats; A.J. Hackett Bungy; West Arm Power Station; Fuji; Hanimex; PCL Colour Labs; Brits: New Zealand; AA; Seitz Phototechnik.

Tim Snowdon

Introduction

Imagine you are standing at a beautiful view point. Wherever you look the view is breathtaking. You turn around, soaking up the panorama in front, to the side and even behind you. Then you lift your camera, focus, and...experience a huge amount of frustration. You just can't capture the view, because it is literally all around you. Taking a normal photograph of any majestic vista is a bit like looking at just one part of a great painting.

Now imagine a camera that can actually spin around in circles, sweeping round to capture everything you can see! That is exactly what the remarkable Seitz Roundshot does, allowing the photographer to take full 360° photographs. This book contains 60 of these true panoramic photographs, which capture the breathtaking diversity of scenery in New Zealand as no ordinary camera can.

The Seitz Roundshot is an exceptional example of Swiss engineering. When a photograph is taken the top part of the camera body, including the lens, rotates, while the film in the camera travels in the opposite direction. The moving image from the lens is projected through a narrow opening in front of the film. The film is synchronised to move past this opening at precisely the same speed as the image moves. It can take as little as 1.5 seconds for a complete rotation, and the resulting photographs are truly unique.

The Seitz Roundshot camera literally spins around, and photographs everything you can see in a complete circle!

Surprisingly, this is not a new invention. The first rotating panoramic cameras were made about 100 years ago, and operated on exactly the same principle. The science involved is relatively simple, the precision engineering required is not.

The amount of rotation required for each photo is set by a remote hand controller before the exposure is started; this may range from 90° to 810° (two and a quarter circles), so it is possible to have the same point appearing twice in one photo!

Using this camera you can appear twice in the same photograph. This picture covers a 400° area.

The main panoramic photographs you will find across the top of each page in this book are all taken with the Seitz Roundshot. They range from a complete 360° circle down to a minimum of 200°.

These photographs should not be confused with the more common 'panoramic format' photographs. The latter are, in fact, normal wide angle photographs (80–90° angle of view) with the top and bottom of the image cut off, sometimes called a 'letter box' format.

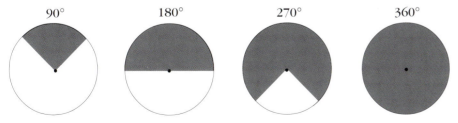

The common panoramic photographs only view a 90° angle. In this book, the minimum angle filmed is 180°, and the maximum is a complete circle, 360°. The centre of the circle represents the position of the camera.

When you travel to the locations shown in this book you will find that you have to turn your head, or maybe even your whole body, to see everything that appears in the photograph. It will literally be all around you, not just one small part of the view. It is important to remember that these pictures are in fact circles, or semi-circles, that have been flattened out.

When putting this book together I wanted it to achieve three goals. Firstly, to capture the outstanding beauty and diversity of New Zealand. Secondly, to produce a practical souvenier for people travelling through the country. Thirdly, to appeal to photography enthusiasts. The last goal was most probably the easiest, as true panoramic photographs are so rare.

To make this book as user-friendly as possible, each panoramic photograph is accompanied by a certain amount of information. A map reference number allows you to find the location of the panorama on the maps of the North and South Island at the end of the book.

The angle of view of each panoramic photograph is indicated by a symbol, as well as the actual angle, so you can easily visualise how much of a circle you are seeing. The viewer is in the centre of the circle, the blacked out area represents how much of the complete circle can be seen.

Each panorama is accompanied by text highlighting the local history and mythology of the area. Where specific features in the photographs are mentioned in the text, they are indicated by reference numbers under the appropriate point of the panorama.

Each page also has another photograph taken in the same area as the main panorama, or on a similar theme. These may be normal format photos or smaller true panoramas.

Because of the incredible angle of view encompassed by these photographs I feel they are a very true record of New Zealand, and are thus of great archival interest. Imagine how fascinating it will be to go to the featured locations in 25 or 100 years, and to be able to see exactly what New Zealand looked like at the end of the second millennium. How will erosion have affected the rural areas? Will the towns and cities be recognisable?

To have the privilege of spending eight months photographing New Zealand from Cape Reinga to Bluff is a remarkable opportunity. To have seen locations as diverse as White Island and Napier, or Franz Joseph Glacier and the Canterbury Plains, is something we will never forget. At times the photography for this book seemed like a marathon task that would never be finished — usually when we were watching the next day's gloomy weather forecast! Despite this we never lost our sense of wonder at what we were seeing. Locations such as the Tasman Glacier, Milford Sound, Lake Wakatipu, Mount Ruapehu and the Te Mata Hills were places that moved us with their unspoilt beauty. The towns and cities presented us with a fascinating mixture of modern, vibrant life, and a sense of the spirit of the pioneers — Maori and pakeha — who sailed the oceans to reach this tiny, but most beautiful, country.

Taking your own panorama

Even though you need a true rotating panoramic camera to take seamless photographs like those in this book, you can create interesting panoramas with a normal SLR camera, and to a lesser extent with a compact camera. To take such a photograph two things are essential:

1. A tripod with a head that swivels horizontally. Mark the part of the head which does not rotate with twelve equally spaced markers (think of the face of a clock), so you can measure how far you have turned your camera horizontally.

2 A camera which can lock the exposure given to the film so that it is the same for each photo taken for the panorama.

To take your own panorama do the following:
1. Place your camera on a level tripod.
2. Use a 35mm lens if you have an SLR.
3. Set the exposure to the correct level for the most important part of the scene. This exposure should be kept the same for each photo taken. Try to take the photo when the sun is high in the sky to avoid flare.
4. Decide on your starting place and point the camera in this direction.
5. Take note of where your camera is in relation to the twelve markers you have put on your tripod.
6. Take a photo.
7. Rotate the camera one-twelfth of a turn, using your markers as a guide. Take another photo.
8. Do this twelve times to complete a full circle.

When you get the prints back, you will need to cut the overlapping part of the photos off, and then mount the remainder on card.

CAPE REINGA, NORTHLAND

1   2

Kai Hawaiki noa atu ahau e noho atu.
I am sitting far away in Hawaiki.

There are not many places on Earth where you can see an ocean and a sea meet as they do at Columbia Bank (3). It's a wonderful sensation, standing at the top of New Zealand, contemplating the vastness of the ocean around you, and watching the weather change before your eyes.

Cape Reinga (1) is a wild and windy spot, and it is easy to imagine why it is the legendary point of departure of Maori souls returning to their mythical homeland of Hawaiki. The spirits were believed to travel up the west coast along Ninety Mile Beach to this westerly point of Spirits Bay then to descend the cape to an old pohutukawa tree and leap into the sea (the name Reinga translates as Place of Leaping). Once in the sea, doors of kelp parted for the spirits to show the way to the next life, although a last breath could be taken at Three Kings Islands before leaving this world. After a battle, it was said that the numerous souls of the dead sounded like a flock of birds passing overhead.

Cape Maria van Diemen (2) was named by the explorer Abel Tasman on 5 January 1643, after the wife of the Governor of Batavia. In good weather you can see the Three Kings Islands — also named by Tasman on the eve of Epiphany — on the horizon. Tasman reported seeing people on the islands 'of very large size, taking prodigious long strides', but they have been uninhabited since 1840.

The lighthouse (4) was installed at Cape Reinga in 1941, a light having been in place on nearby Motuopao Island since 1879.

340°

Lighthouse
Don't miss the signpost by the lighthouse giving you the distance to places as far away as London, 19,271 km, and Tokyo, a relatively close 8831 km!

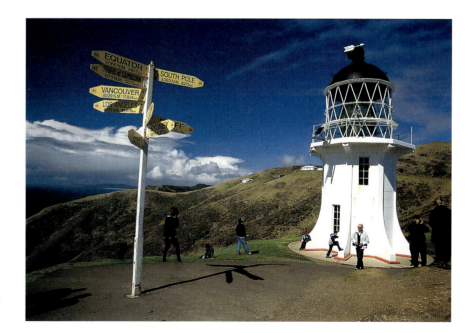

KERIKERI, NORTHLAND

1   2

In them days it was about as bad as dyin", to come out to the Colonies.

Blanche Baugham

Surprisingly, the oldest wooden and the oldest stone building in New Zealand are right next to each other. All of the buildings on this page were part of the Church Missionary Society's second mission station in New Zealand. The ship *General Gates* brought Samuel Marsden, Francis Hall, Reverend John Butler, and James Kemp and his family to establish the mission in 1819. The land was donated by Nga Puhi chief Hongi Hika, who also offered his protection to the fledgling settlement.

The Stone Store (1) was seldom used for its original purpose, although the name persists. From 1842 to 1844 part of the top floor was occupied by the library of New Zealand's first Anglican bishop, George Selwyn, who would walk 16 km from Waimate North to use his books. During the period of conflict with Hone Heke Pokai of the Nga Puhi, the building was used as an ammunition store. It is now owned by the New Zealand Historic Places Trust.

As you drive down towards the Stone Store, St James' Church is perched on the hill to your right. The first school-cum-chapel was built in 1829 at the heart of the settlement, to be replaced by another chapel in 1829. The existing St. James' was built in 1878.

Wooden Kemp House (2), sited on the banks of the Kerikeri River (3) is the oldest surviving building in New Zealand; it is well worth looking around as it retains many of its original fittings. It was built for John Butler and his family, who lived here for two years, and was later occupied by other mission staff. In 1832 it passed to James Kemp, blacksmith and lay missioner, and remained in his family for 142 years. In 1974 the family gave the house to the nation.

295°

Map ref. [2]

St. James' Church
The Kemp family are buried in the church yard of St James'.

Russell, Bay of Islands

1 2

The beautiful natural setting of Russell is complemented by the fine colonial buildings along the waterfront, such as the Duke of Marlborough Hotel (1) shown here.

The first hotel on the site was built by ex-convict John Johnson, who bought the land in 1827. The Duke of Marlborough was the first licensed public house in New Zealand. The original building was burnt down in 1845 by Hone Heke, who chopped down the British flagpole in the town four times as a sign of his contempt for British rule, before engaging British forces. The second and third buildings were also destroyed by fire, in 1875 and 1931, respectively.

The fourth and current hotel, situated just next to the original site, was moved here in 1931 from Cable Bay, where it had been the Women's Accommodation Block of the Cable Station.

Russell stands on the site of an abandoned Maori settlement called Kororareka. By the 1830s Kororareka was so notorious for the wild living of the whalers, adventurers and ex-convicts who frequented it, that it was known as 'the hell-hole of the Pacific'. Grog shops lined the now peaceful Strand (2) where the Duke of Marlborough stands. A liquor licence was not necessary until 1840, when British law was introduced following the signing of the Treaty of Waitangi.

The original Russell was established as the capital of New Zealand, 7 km south of Kororareka, by the first Lieutenant-Governor of New Zealand, Captain William Hobson. Little construction had been carried out before the capital was transferred to Auckland in 1840. In 1844 the name Russell was adopted by the township of Kororareka.

350°

Map ref. [3]

The Treaty House, Waitangi
The Treaty of Waitangi was signed on the lawn in front of this simple house on 6 February 1840 by Captain William Hobson and 45 Maori chiefs.

View from Mount Victoria, Auckland

1   2

There are harbours and small eruptions and flares of landscape with the odd distant domes of volcanoes under the sky.

Peter Wells

The Hauraki Gulf, between the mainland and the Coromandel Peninsula, is studded with over a hundred named islands, large and small. These islands are relics of the hills and volcanoes of an ancient countryside, drowned by the sea.

Rangitoto Island (1), which lies to the north-east of the mouth of the Waitemata Harbour, erupted out of the sea 600–800 years ago. From a distance, Rangitoto appears covered in dense bush, but a visit to it reveals that it is still in the process of being colonised by indigenous flora. There is, as yet, no soil on the island, just scoria and lava rock. As everywhere, lichens, then mosses, were the pioneering species; subsequently, over 200 other species of plants, including many ferns, have colonised the island. Pohutukawa have established themselves by rooting in crevices in the rock; they are now so plentiful that 8 tonnes of pohutukawa honey is harvested on the island annually.

North Head (2), only 1200 m away from Mount Victoria (4), stands at the north side of the entrance to the Waitemata Harbour. It is the site of military fortifications of both Maori and European origin. Above ground it is ridged with Maori earthworks and defaced by modern naval buildings, while underground it is riddled with a labyrinth of tunnels. Its life as a European fort began in the 1860s, and gun emplacements were installed in 1885 against a perceived Russian threat. The head was fortified until 1959, and stories still circulate of secret tunnels hiding ammunitions stores and other remnants of World War II. Today, only a small area of the hill remains in naval hands, the rest, including some tunnels, being open to the public as part of the Hauraki Gulf Maritime Park.

335°

3 4 Map ref. [4]

Mount Victoria, capped by a harbour signal station, is one of two remaining volcanoes in Devonport (3) on Auckland's North Shore, two lesser cones having been quarried away. The early European settlement of Flagstaff, which grew up on the west side of Mount Victoria, was eventually incorporated into the Borough of Devonport, constituted in 1886. Like its namesake in the southwest of England, Devonport is a naval base, although of a more genteel nature than the historic British port.

North Head from Cheltenham Beach
At low tide the sea retreats into the distance, leaving a vast expanse of sand with only the shallowest covering of water.

City of Lights, Auckland

1

2

Ka tuhi te toto o Kaitangata.
The blood of Kaitangata is gleaming.

Like many modern cities, Auckland takes on an almost magical quality at dusk. This shot was taken in the five minutes between sunset and darkness when the clouds took on an almost luminescent quality, which contrasts so well with the warmth of Restaurant 360° (1).

New Zealand's largest city was also once the capital of the young colony. In 1840, after the signing of the Treaty of Waitangi, Governor Hobson moved the capital south from Russell to an area of fertile land with two excellent harbours. The new town developed in a piecemeal fashion as, unlike Wellington, Christchurch and Dunedin, it was not a planned settlement. In 1865, the honour of capital city was transferred to Wellington, but Auckland has since gained dominance of the country's economy.

Auckland City is built on a narrow isthmus between the Waitemata and Manukau harbours. The Waitemata is the home of New Zealand's largest port, and enormous container ships are an everyday sight for the people of Auckland. At its outer reaches, the Waitemata Harbour is spanned by the Auckland Harbour Bridge (2), 1020 m long and opened in 1959.

From Mount Eden (3) you can see the whole isthmus of Auckland with its bays and hills, and it is clear that volcanoes and the sea are major influences on the topography of the city. Like many of Auckland's volcanoes, Mount Eden is the site of an old Maori pa, with terracing and storage pits still visible.

310°

3   Map ref. [4]

Sunrise over Rangitoto
An unusual feature of this almost circular island is that its outline appears the same from almost every part of the city.

Waterfront, Auckland

1

2

In the Auckland of the 1990s, the buildings have come right down to the waterfront, to spend the day gazing at their reflections in the sea beneath them.

Ferries for the numerous islands near Auckland and the picturesque North Shore suburb of Devonport leave from their berths beside the Ferry Building (2). This lovely building, opened in 1912, was restored in 1988 and houses shops, cafés and offices, as well as the ferry terminal. Ferries have been a vital link between the city and the North Shore since the last century, but the need for a bridge across the Waitemata Harbour was long recognised. Despite a Commission on the subject in 1929, it was another 30 years before the ferries lost their monopoly on trans-harbour transport.

The ferry berths nestle between two larger wharves, Queens (1) and Princes (4) wharves. Princes Wharf is Auckland's major passenger liner dock, with easy access to downtown hotels and shops, and also houses the distinctive Ports of Auckland building (3). Across the water, Queens Wharf is known particularly for the handling of enormous shipments of Japanese cars, many of them second hand.

A port developed in Auckland during the early settlement days of the 1840s, followed by the establishment of the Auckland Harbour Board by Act of Parliament in 1870. As the port grew in importance, more land was reclaimed from the sea to accommodate the increased number of ships and their cargo. In 1988, the new Ports of Auckland Limited purchased the commercial holdings of the Auckland Harbour Board in Auckland and Onehunga. Auckland is now the country's largest general

220°

cargo port, handling, in monetary terms, around 65 per cent of imports, and is the leading port of export for dairy, beef and wool products.

The Hobson Wharf Maritime Museum was opened in 1993, and spans the breadth of New Zealand's seafaring history, covering more than 1000 years. The museum also has exhibits on the water, such as a massive floating crane, a Maori war canoe and a tiny steam tug.

Maritime Museum
This photograph was taken while a replica of HM Bark *Endeavour* was visiting the Maritime Museum.

MAORI GALLERY, AUCKLAND MUSEUM

1   2

Nga mahi whakairo, nga mahi a Rua.
The art of carving is the art of Rua.

The Maori Gallery at Auckland Museum contains some of the finest remaining examples of ancient Maori carving. Pou whakairo (1), large wooden figures, represent specific tribal ancestors.

Major buildings and canoes were given evocative names: the pataka (2), or raised storehouse, seen here is called Te Puawai-o-Te Arawa, 'The Flower of the Arawa'. This was the property of Te Pokiha Taranui, the leading chief of the Ngati Pikiao tribe. The pataka symbolised the status and power of the chief, and its carved figures represented his genealogy, and that of the tribe. The captain of the Arawa canoe, Tamatekapua, is represented over the doorway.

The whare whakairo (3), or meeting house, seen here is named Hotunui, after an ancestor of the Tainui tribe. The whare was a wedding gift from Ngati Awa chief Apanui Hamaiwaho to his daughter and son-in-law. It took three years to build, being completed in 1878. The building was deposited in Auckland Museum on a loan basis by Erueni Taipari.

Te Toki-a-Tapiri (4) was the last of the great war canoes (waka), cut out of a single totara log to carry 100 warriors. It is named in commemoration of an ancestor of Te Waka Tarakau of Ngati Kahungunu, who commissioned the work in 1836. The partly completed canoe changed hands several times before it was confiscated by the government after the outbreak of war in the Waikato, although compensation was eventually paid to Ngati Te Ata. The Museum received the canoe in 1885.

The Museum is the base for the Pounamu Maori Cultural Group (5), which aims to raise the awareness and interest of domestic and international visitors in aspects of traditional Maori culture. Visitors are greeted with a ritual challenge, then welcomed

260°

3   4   5   Map ref. [4]

once they have demonstrated their peaceful intentions. Maori heritage is illustrated with displays of weaponry, singing, and games and dances aimed at improving both reflexes and eye-hand coordination.

Maori Performers, Rotorua
Maori performers share their culture, followed by a traditional feast (hangi), with visitors to the reconstructed village of Te Tawa Ngahiri Pa, Rotorua.

PIHA BEACH, WEST AUCKLAND

There were few baches...and only marram grass covered the great sand dunes between the land and the sea.

Sandra Coney

On Auckland's west coast the rocky headlands of the Waitakere Ranges are pounded relentlessly by the huge surf of the Tasman Sea. The stark contrast with the gentle seas of the Hauraki Gulf beaches led the Maori to declare the aggressive west coast to be male, while the soft east coast was female. Reaching the west coast beaches means a tortuous journey along the narrow, winding roads that cross the Waitakeres, but many Aucklanders eschew the calm Hauraki Gulf waters for the exhilarating surf of the wild west coast beaches.

In summer Piha comes alive, with crowds pulsating to the beat of live music, and enjoying the party atmosphere. Many of the settlement's 1000 residents are artists and craftspeople, and their numbers are swelled by the surfers who come to ride the rolling breakers.

Piha means 'ripple at the bow of a canoe', a name that still has relevance, since kayaks ride the surf these days. It is a popular beach for surfing and fishing, but this is a treacherous coast that has claimed many lives — fishermen swept off rocks and swimmers carried out to sea. An active surf lifesaving club strives to reduce these tragedies.

Lion Rock (1), sitting astride the mouth of the Piha Stream, dominates the beach. A steep climb to the summit of the Rock, once a headland, affords sweeping views over the beach and surrounding hills and out to sea. In the distance, Te Waha Point (2) juts out, like the snout of a crocodile sniffing the surf.

At the south end of the beach, the Tasman Track covers the short distance to the Gap and associated blowhole, a fine sight in heavy seas.

265°

1   2   Map ref. [5]

Black Volcanic Sand
This shot, taken between Lion Rock and Te Waha Point, shows clearly the wonderful colour contrast created by the black volcanic sand, the grass, the hills and the sky.

Mare's Leg Cove, Coromandel

The walk to these beaches through the Cathedral Cove Reserve, on the east coast of the Coromandel Peninsula, near Hahei, passes through pohutukawa groves and takes in spectacular sea views.

The Coromandel Peninsula is a mountainous, forest-covered area with a climate moderated by the influence of the sea. In some places the coast consists of golden, sandy beaches, in others the waves crash against jagged rocks and forbidding cliffs. The bush hides the relics of early exploitation: kauri log dams, saw pits and decaying mining machinery.

The area was ravaged by logging, gum digging, mining and unproductive farming. Once, the area was covered by huge kauri forests, but these were depleted from the beginning of the nineteenth century. Today, there are large tracts of exotic *Pinus radiata* plantations, and much of the vegetation on the hills is scrub which will take many decades to regenerate into mature native forest. Despite these ravages, the overall impression is a land of green, bush-covered ranges surrounded by a sparkling sea.

The Cathedral Cove Reserve protects three bays which are separated by high cliffs. At low tide it is possible to walk through a cavernous hole in the rock that separates Mare's Leg Cove from Cathedral Cove. The view of the islands in the Bay of Plenty is even better from the cliff tops of the Reserve.

The relentless surging of the sea has slowly sculpted the base of Mare's Leg Rock (1) so it now balances precariously, as if on a pre-historic pedestal.

235°

Map ref. [6]

Sail Rock, Cathedral Cove
This rock is even more impressive than Mare's Leg Rock, towering over the beach like the sail of a tall ship.

WAIOTAHI RESERVE, BAY OF PLENTY

The Bay of Plenty has dozens of wonderful beaches which are relatively quiet even in summer. This area has a very high proportion of sunny days and mild weather all year round.

The Bay of Plenty was named by Captain James Cook in 1769. He found the coast to be populated with thriving Maori settlements where the people were well disposed to supply provisions. This was a stark contrast to his reception at Poverty Bay a few weeks earlier.

The Waiotahi River rises to the north of the Kahikatea Range and flows northwards to reach the Bay of Plenty here at the Waiotahi Reserve. In this sheltered inlet, wading birds thrive and local people gather shellfish.

At the western end of nearby Waiotahi Beach is The Gateway, carved by Graham Hayward to commemorate the 150th anniversary of the signing of the Treaty of Waitangi. The Maori name Te Ara-ki-te-Rawhiti (The Pathway to the Sunrise), symbolises the unity of the people of New Zealand as they move forward to the future. The carving depicts the landing in this area of Tarawa, ancestor of the Whakatohea people, and his brother Tuwharanui. It also has figures denoting the intermingling of many races.

One of the most rewarding times to visit the Bay of Plenty is December, when the many thousands of pohutukawa trees are covered with their vibrant red blossoms, a beautiful alternative to the traditional Christmas tree.

310°

Map ref. [7]

Christ Church, Raukokore
Christ Church was built in 1894 by Duncan Stirling, who is credited with many churches in the area. He subsequently married a local Whanau-a-Apanui girl here. Stirling had no architectural training, but still produced a well proportioned building, with this example made more striking by its water's edge setting.

White Island

1   2

With steam hissing out of gas vents, bubbling mud pools and a desolate landscape, White Island is a unique experience.

Captain Cook so named this place in 1769 because of the dense clouds of white steam hanging over it. The crater is continually active and ash showers occur frequently. Great care is needed when walking around the island, as in places there may be only a thin crust over a thermal area.

This small island comprises three volcanic cones, the highest of which, Mount Ngatoro, is 321 m. The crater itself (2), however, lies only a few metres above sea level. The crater lake is visible on some days, but on others it is covered in a pall of steam. The walk to the crater is never without reward: you cross the eerie island landscape, moving between steamy pools and yellow, sulphur-rimmed gas vents (1). The jets of steam hissing from the ground contain both sulphur dioxide and hydrochloric acid, making a prolonged visit an exercise in olfactory endurance.

In the past, a number of attempts have been made to extract gypsum and sulphur from the island on a commercial basis. In 1913 there was a marked increase in volcanic activity; the following year a group of eleven men was killed by a violent lahar which swept most of the mining settlement out to sea.

The activity of the volcano is continually monitored by several government and university departments, not only for academic interest, but because a major eruption could devastate low lying areas of the Bay of Plenty.

Several operators run trips to White Island, which is 50 km off the coast from Whakatane. The island is a privately owned scenic reserve and bird sanctuary for which a landing fee is charged in aid of a charity.

The waters around the island have an abundance of marine life, including dolphins and sharks. The deep waters of the nearby White Island Trench, the warm Auckland

325°

Map ref. [8]

current and the thermal activity of the volcano itself, all contribute to this profusion of fish.

Sulphur Works
This decaying factory building, which once belonged to White Island Products Limited, was in use up to 1934.

Agrodome Farm, Rotorua

See him coming in from the back country at mustering-time with a mob of two thousand or so and his dogs handling each woolly as though its fleece was worth its weight in gold...

O.E. Middleton

When Captain Cook introduced the first sheep, albeit unsuccessfully, into New Zealand, he could not have known how prophetic an action it was. Today, sheep outnumber people by thirty to one, and scenes such as that above are close to the heart of every New Zealander.

Early exports were limited to wool, mainly from the Merino, a single-purpose wool-producing breed introduced from Australia in 1840. In 1882 the first refrigerated ship, *Dunedin,* left Port Chalmers with a cargo of frozen meat bound for Britain, opening up the export market for perishable goods. This led to the introduction of dual-purpose breeds such as the Romney, which still dominates the national flock. It also allowed the expansion of both dairy and beef farming, to complement sheep raising. Further technological advances, such as aerial top-dressing, led to improved pasture quality and hence allowed higher stocking levels.

The success of sheep farming in New Zealand owes much to its sheepdogs — the collies, huntaways and heading dogs. Each type of dog has its own strengths and expertise, making it useful in a particular situation. It takes four to six months to train a sheep dog, which will then have a working life of around ten years, more if the terrain is flat. The skill and boundless energy of the dogs, and their rapport with the shepherd, are a joy to see, and a source of amazement to the city dweller.

A good shearer can shear 300–350 sheep a day for several months a year. With electric shears operating at high speed, the skill and accuracy of the shearer are essential. Unevenness of cutting reduces the value of the staple of wool, and any

Map ref. [9]

wool not sheared on the first pass is of little value. The founder of the Agrodome, W. Godfrey Bowen, a champion shearer himself, pioneered a training scheme for sheep shearers in New Zealand and, subsequently, in other parts of the world.

Stockhandling
The flock seen here is part of the Agrodome Farm, near Rotorua, which has daily demonstrations of sheep shearing, and sheepdog trials.

Pohutu Geyser, Rotorua

1

...sometimes, higher than the tallest forest tree, a sleek shining panel of hot water shot into the air, caressing the sun.

Ngahuia Te Awekotuku

Whakarewarewa Thermal Reserve (1) is probably the most famous of Rotorua's thermal areas, containing the largest geyser in New Zealand, Pohutu (2), which can reach 31 m. Pohutu, aptly, means 'big splash' or 'explosion'. When we visited the Pohutu geyser it was erupting every 15 minutes or so, but this can vary quite a lot. When it does erupt the ground vibrates with the force of it.

Whakarewarewa Thermal Reserve has more than 500 hot springs welling up in an area measuring only 1 km by 500 m. The whole reserve has a fascinating, alien feel to it, rather like a science fiction movie set. Steam issues from the ground, adding to the drama of the place. The springs may surface as clear water, in the form of geysers if they are chloride springs, or boiling mud if they are sulphate springs. Geysers occur when superheated water, containing dissolved carbon dioxide, collects below the surface of rocks; when the increasing vapour pressure reaches a critical point the steam is forced out through narrow cracks in the rock.

The land around Rotorua was originally settled in the fourteenth century by descendants of the voyagers on the Arawa canoe. Whakarewarewa was one of their principal settlements. In 1823 the lands of Te Arawa were invaded by Hongi Hika, the Ngapuhi chief from Kerikeri, who had the advantage of muskets. The Tuhorangi sub-tribe of Te Arawa was displaced by the eruption of Mount Tarawera in 1886, and now occupies a site at the edge of the thermal reserve.

260°

2   Map ref. [9]

Tudor Bathhouse, Rotorua
Set in the very English Government Gardens, the Tudor Bathhouse is the location of an excellent art and history museum, featuring information on the local Te Arawa tribe, past volcanic activity and the famous Pink and White Terraces. The bathhouse was built in 1906 in the fashion of the famous European spas.

Aranui Cave, Waitomo

Of all sizes and the most fantastic shapes, they gleamed around us, as though the spirits of the dead, summoned from their long sleep, were bursting the chrysalis of the tomb.

William Satchell

Although less visited and smaller than the famous glow-worm caves of Waitomo, we found Aranui Cave the more impressive.

The Aranui, Waitomo and Raukuri caves are just part of a large system, of which 85 km of passages and caverns have been explored. The caves occur in an area of limestone. Water, which contains dissolved atmospheric carbon dioxide and is hence slightly acidic, seeps through from the surface, and erodes away the limestone.

As the fissures increase in size, the trickles of water become underground streams which cut out channels that eventually become caves. Drips of water containing dissolved limestone evaporate, leaving the limestone deposits that form stalactites and stalagmites at an imperceptible rate — one cubic inch every 300–500 years.

Aranui Cave was discovered in 1910 by Te Ruruku Aranui while he was hunting a pig, which he killed in the entrance to the cave. Te Ruruku Aranui was paid £20 for his discovery, and the cave was officially opened in 1911. One of the most interesting formations here is the Beehive stalagmite (1). Today, viewing platforms (2) protect these delicate structures.

The Waitomo caves were known to generations of Maori, but they would not enter owing to their fear of evil spirits. However, in 1887 Fred Mace, a surveyor, persuaded chief Tane Tinorau to accompany him on a journey by raft into the caves. They explored for some time, expecting to emerge on the other side of the hill where the river resurfaced. Finding their way blocked by a large bank of driftwood, they struggled back against the stream, nearing the entrance just as their candles

270°

Map ref. [10]

failed. Visitors began flocking to the caves; the canny Tane Tinorau realised he had a tourist asset on his tribal lands and began guiding people through the caves for an entrance fee.

Marokopa Falls
The Marokopa River arises in the hills west of Waitomo Caves and crosses the Waitomo District to reach the North Taranaki Bight near Marokopa. These beautiful 54 m falls are near Te Anga.

KINLOCH, LAKE TAUPO

This shot was taken from within the overhanging branches of a willow tree, a lovely tranquil location.

Kinloch was the home of Sir Keith Holyoake, who was the New Zealand Prime Minister during the 1960s. There is a monument commemorating him at the headland lookout over Lake Taupo, and many local roads were named after members of his family.

Kinloch marina (1) was built in the 1960s from reclaimed raupo swamp, and joins Lake Taupo at its northern shore.

Lake Taupo itself covers more than 600 km², and lies at an altitude of 396 m, in the geographical centre of the North Island. It occupies a series of volcanic depressions, formed in eruptions so powerful that the atmospheric effects are reported to have been noted in China and Rome around A.D.186. The lake is part of a volcanic zone which stretches from Tongariro National Park to White Island in the Bay of Plenty.

Lake Taupo and its surrounding rivers are renowned the world over for their trout fishing. Brown trout eggs of British stock were introduced to New Zealand from Tasmania in 1868, and Californian rainbow trout in 1884. Gradually, trout from hatcheries were introduced all over the country and thrived in the lakes and rivers of New Zealand. Hatcheries still play an important role in stocking areas where there are no suitable spawning grounds. The country's rainbow trout are all descended from that first shipment and represent the world's only remaining pure strain.

325°

Map ref. [11]

Lake Taupo
Lake Taupo and its rivers are a fisherman's paradise, providing some of the best trout fishing in the world. Since it is illegal to sell trout in New Zealand, the only way to eat one is to catch it yourself. This shot was taken from Acacia Bay, on the northern shore of the lake.

Mount Ruapehu

One week after this photograph was taken in late 1995, this whole area was covered in grey ash. In a series of eruptions that caught the attention of people around the world, Mount Ruapehu reminded skiers that this is more than just a lump of inert rock.

Tongariro was New Zealand's first National Park, and one of the first in the world. Rather than see the sacred volcanic mountains of Ruapehu (2), Ngauruhoe and Tongariro exploited and despoiled, the paramount chief of the Tuwharetoa tribe, Te Heuheu Tukino, gave the land to the nation in 1887 'for the purposes of a national park'. Such it became by Act of Parliament in 1894.

Mount Ruapehu, at 2792 m, is the highest mountain in the North Island; it is also an active volcano, having significant eruptions every 30–50 years. Early eruptions occurred northwest of the present summit, the remnants of that volcano being visible as Pinnacle Ridge to the northeast of the Whakapapa Valley (1). The current summit is broad, with at least two craters, one of which is active. Below its circle of peaks is Crater Lake, full of steaming, sulphurous water.

At one time the lower slopes of Mount Ruapehu were entirely forested, but trees are now confined to the southern and western areas. There are some stands of rimu containing specimens about 600 years old; other stands are dominated by mountain beech or red beech.

Mount Ruapehu attracts large numbers of visitors each year to its three ski fields, Whakapapa, Turoa and Tukino. The Staircase in the Whakapapa Valley ski area was formed by lava flows from Mount Ruapehu.

305°

1   2   Map ref. [**12**]

Mount Ruapehu in Winter
The upper peaks of Ruapehu wear their winter white mantle all year round, belying the fiery heat beneath the mountain.

THE GRAND CHATEAU, MOUNT RUAPEHU

The Grand Chateau (2), in the Tongariro National Park, is one of the most well known buildings in New Zealand, but this image of it rising out of the mist on a frosty morning is less familiar.

The Grand Chateau was built in 1929, inspired by the Prime Minister, Gordon Coates, who had a vision of developing an outstanding international resort in the Tongariro National Park. The Tongariro Park Tourist Company was formed to develop both the hotel and an alpine resort to complement it.

The hotel was later owned by the government, and during World War II it served as a hospital. Volcanic eruptions in 1945 led to its evacuation. It was renovated and reopened in 1948, after Mount Ruapehu (3) and the Tongariro National Park had been designated a World Heritage Park.

In the background the classic volcanic cone of Mount Ngauruhoe (1), the most continuously active volcano in New Zealand, can just be distinguished, as it rises out of the morning mist. According to Maori tradition, Ngatoro-i-rangi, the priest and navigator of the Arawa canoe, journeyed inland and climbed Mount Tongariro to lay claim to all the land he could view from the summit. A great snowstorm came, and on the point of freezing to death, Ngatoro-i-rangi prayed that the gods would send fire to warm him. The gods sent the fire underground from the homeland of Hawaiki, but on the way it broke through to the surface at White Island, Rotorua, Tarawera, Orakei Korako and Taupo, creating the thermal areas. Eventually, the fire poured out of Mount Tongariro, forming a new crater on its flanks. The grateful navigator threw his slave Auruhoe into the crater as an offering to the gods, and thus Ngauruhoe was formed and named.

260°

2   3   Map ref. [12]

Tawhai Falls
These attractive falls, just 4 km from the Grand Chateau, are popular with canoeists and sightseers alike.

Mount Taranaki

1   2   3

...certainly the noblest hill I have ever seen.

Joseph Banks

Mount Taranaki (3) is one of the loveliest of New Zealand's mountains, standing in isolation without peer or rival. The almost perfect symmetry of its volcanic cone is marred only by the subsidiary cone of Fantham's Peak. The mountain is often shrouded in heavy cloud and must have been so when Abel Tasman sailed along this coast in December 1642, because, although he recorded Cape Egmont, he made no mention of this dominant feature. Captain Cook named it Mount Egmont on 10 January 1770, after a First Lord of the Admiralty, but the ancient Maori name received official recognition in 1986.

It is said that Taranaki originally dwelled in the centre of the North Island with the other mountains, but was banished after a duel with Tongariro over the love of the beautiful Pihanga. Taranaki retreated, carving out the Whanganui River and other features as he went. While Taranaki was resting, the Pouakai Range threw out a spur, capturing the mountain, which remains there weeping for his lost love.

The higher regions of the mountain, a place of burial for chiefs and tohunga, were tapu to the Maori, who believed them to be inhabited by the ngarara, mythological reptiles. The first ascent is attributed to Tahurangi in around 1420, and wisps of cloud clinging to the summit are said to be Te Ahi-a-Tahurangi, 'the fire of Tahurangi'. The first recorded ascent was by Dr Ernest Dieffenbach and James Heberley in 1839. Their guides would climb no further than the snowline, but remained to pray that the Europeans would come to no harm in the tapu territory.

A dormant volcano, Mount Taranaki was formed around 70,000 years ago, and its most recent eruption is believed to have taken place in 1775. The last great eruption was around 1665, a date estimated from the change in the annual growth rings of

Map ref. [13]

ancient kaikawaka trees, still alive despite having been inundated with ash in that year.

Other prominent peaks seen in this panorama include Maude Peak (1), 1220 m, Henry Peak (2), 1222 m, and the Hump (4), 1226 m.

Lake Mangamahoe
The water from this artificial lake is piped for nearly 1.25 km to a hydroelectric power station, as well as furnishing the New Plymouth water supply.

Te Mata Hills, Hawke's Bay

1

The mountains are the ridged backbone of a whale plunging. The landscape is the turmoiled waves of its huge tail flukes descending.

Witi Ihimaera

This very impressive valley climbs out of the relative flatness of the southern end of Hawke's Bay. In Maori legend, local chiefs wanted to rid themselves of the giant Te Mata, so they encouraged him to fall in love with a beautiful girl. At their behest, she then set him a series of tasks to win her love, the last of which proved fatal. In his attempt to eat through the mountain range behind Havelock North, he choked and died. The outline of the peak is the profile of the fallen chief.

The 98 hectare Te Mata Park includes the 399 m high Te Mata Peak (1), which rises above dramatic cliffs to command an extensive view. In good conditions you can see not only the whole of Hawke's Bay, but also Mount Ruapehu in the Tongariro National Park. The view over the peaceful Tukituki River (2) is a contrast to its name, meaning 'to demolish'.

The sheer drop and updraughts from the ocean make this a favourite launch pad for hang-gliders. Walkers can take the Te Mata Peak Walkway along the ridgeline. The valley is a good area for cycling, particularly on the far side of the Tukituki River, where the hills are manageable and the views superb. Really proficient mountain bikers can cycle up the road to Te Mata Peak then back down a hair-raising track.

Hawke's Bay, the inland area which spreads out below the Te Mata Hills, is a region of fruit growing. The canneries and freezing plants of Hastings are kept busy processing the local produce, while the area's wineries are occupied with the fruit of the vine.

Hawke Bay was named after Sir Edward Hawke, the First Lord of the Admiralty, by Captain James Cook in 1769.

360°

2   Map ref. [14]

Te Mata Peak View
Recent rain has left the grass beautifully lush and green in this photo.
The hill in this picture is the one from which I took the panorama above.

Mission Vineyards, Hawke's Bay

1

2

Hawke's Bay is the home of some of the finest vineyards in New Zealand. It would take you weeks to visit them all, but what a holiday you would have!

Hawke's Bay has a warm, relatively dry climate ideally suited to the cultivation of vines. The Mission Estate is the oldest and one of the most famous vineyards in the country, and has regular guided tours and tastings.

The beautiful Mission Estate building (1) in this picture was once the Mount St Mary Seminary, built in 1880 for the training of Marist priests and brothers in New Zealand. The seminary was transferred to this site from Meeanee in 1910. The chapel (2) was added in 1933, after the Napier earthquake. French missionaries had been growing grapes for communion wine at Meeanee for many years, and brought their vines here with the seminary (3). The Brothers of the Society of Mary still manage the vineyards, and all profits go to their work in New Zealand and overseas.

The first vines in New Zealand were planted at Kerikeri in 1819 for the Reverend Samuel Marsden, but winemaking was really pioneered by James Busby, the British Resident in the Bay of Islands in 1833. He had developed a love of wine in France in his youth, and had taken this enthusiasm with him first to Australia and then to New Zealand.

The wine industry was scourged by the aphid *Phylloxera* in the 1890s, with the result that all the vines had to be destroyed and replaced with American rootstock. The temperance movement and the Depression of the 1930s hindered the development of the industry, but it is now one of the success stories of world viticulture. In particular, New Zealand's white wines have the reputation of being some of the finest on the international scene.

310°

3 Map ref. [14]

Te Mata Estate
This dramatic house and its vineyard are at the foot of the Te Mata hills. The Te Mata Estate is the oldest commercial winery in the country.

Art Deco Napier

1   2

There was the most terrible shaking. It just went on and on. My only thought was that it was the end of the world.

Mona Hillson

On the morning of 3 February 1931 a two and a half minute earthquake, measuring 7.8 on the Richter scale, destroyed much of Napier and Hastings, killing 256 people. The resulting fires compounded the damage.

HMS *Veronica* was in port at the time and her crew were among the many dedicated rescuers who worked amidst the ruins. The bell of *Veronica* was hung on the new Marine Parade and is rung every New Year to commemorate the efforts of the crew. One of the results of the upheaval was the raising of the harbour bed which provided 4000 hectares of new land for suburbs, industrial areas and an airport.

Out of this disaster a real gem emerged. Most of the rebuilding that took place was done between 1931 and 1933 in the then current Art Deco style, creating one of the highest concentrations of Art Deco buildings in the world. Many of the buildings which survived the disaster were those recently built of reinforced concrete, which also evinced the Art Deco style. The new buildings were designed with more earthquake resistance, but it is to be hoped that they never face a test as severe as that which destroyed the old city. One of the classic examples of these buildings is the Countrywide Bank (1), which was originally a hotel. The most famous street in Napier is Emerson Street (2) which contains numerous examples of fine Art Deco buildings.

The Art Deco style is still actively pursued by today's residents of Napier — some even drive 1930s cars! An Art Deco weekend is held each February when balls, dinners and other events are held, with many people wearing 1930s dress.

Map ref. [15]

Art Deco Art
This mural, just off Emerson Street, continues the Art Deco theme.

Castle Point, Wairarapa

1   2

This gem of a bay is a little off the beaten track, but is definitely worth a visit.

Captain Cook named Castle Point in 1770 as the rock formation seemed to him like a fortress, although time, earthquakes and the elements appear to have reduced it in stature. The eponymous rock is not that on which the lighthouse (2) stands, but lies on the other side of the tidal lagoon formed by the sweep of Castle Point Reef as it arcs southwestwards from the lighthouse.

The 23 m high lighthouse was actually made in England, and was first lit at Castle Point in 1913, when a kerosene lamp was used. It is now an important automatic light for shipping, and its beam can be seen for 48 km. It is the first sight of land for ships sailing to New Zealand from South America. A wooden walkway (1) has been built over the causeway that links the headland to the shore, so access to the lighthouse in no longer dependent on the tide.

Deliverance Cove, the lagoon, is reached through a gap in the Castle Point reef. Missionary William Colenso named the cove in November 1843. He, his fellow passengers and crew tried to row ashore after their ship, *Columbine*, had been driven back from Cook Strait by a storm. They found their way blocked by the reef, but eventually discovered the gap and reached safety in the cove.

It is said that Kupe, the Maori navigator and explorer, tracked a giant octopus to a cave here, and chased it down the coast and through Cook Strait, eventually killing it off the South Island.

A number of fishing boats are based at Castle Point. The Wairarapa coast lacks harbours, so the boats have to be dragged up the beach on trailers to prevent them being pirated by the Pacific Ocean.

315°

3 Map ref. [16]

Rimutaka Summit
The first people to cross the Rimutakas were the Rangitane. It was not until 1841 that these hills were crossed by Europeans, with the aid of two Maori guides. That crossing, led by Robert Stokes and John Child, allowed the Wairarapa to be opened up to settlers.

Cable Car, Wellington

1

Wellington Harbour, the magnificent, the incomparable…it remains a kind of ideal, platonic harbour towards which all others must vainly aspire.

E.H. McCormick

This classic view of Wellington, from the Kelburn terminus of the cable car (2), is given a very different feel by showing the surrounding gardens and buildings.

Wellington has spread over a number of precipitous hills that look down on one of the most beautiful natural harbours in the world. One excellent viewpoint is from the summit of the cable car. A ride from Lambton Quay to the top of the cable car, a 122 m climb, is one of the 'musts' of a visit to Wellington. The cable car service began in 1902 in order to open up for development the suburb of Kelburn, at the top of the line. In 1978 the track was reconstructed using a Swiss system, and the current red cars were introduced, replacing the original ones.

The Botanic Gardens (1), 26 hectares of native and exotic flora, spread from the Kelburn cable car terminus down to Tinakori Road. Here the early European settlers created plantings and buildings nostalgically reminiscent of their Victorian homeland, including the Begonia House and the Lady Norwood Rose Gardens. For generations, Wellingtonians have come here for Sunday afternoon strolls in the serene garden surroundings.

Aside from the tranquil environment, the Botanic Gardens also feature a tea house and the Custodian's Cottage, built in 1876. Within the grounds are also housed the Carter Observatory, the Dominion Observatory, the Geophysics Building and the Meteorological Office. The nearby Bolton Street Memorial Park features the 1857 Sexton's Cottage which was built for the Anglican church by soldiers of the 65th Regiment.

245°

Map ref. [17]

Colonial Villas, Thorndon

Thorndon was the first part of the city to be settled by the New Zealand Company colonists, who left a legacy of delightful wooden villas clinging to the steep hillsides. There are many houses of historical interest here, such as Katherine Mansfield's birthplace at 25 Tinakori Road.

Parliament Buildings, Wellington

1

New Zealand has been governed from this site since 1865 when Wellington became the capital city. A succession of buildings has stood here, some razed to the ground by fire.

Today, the centre of government operations is the distinctive Beehive building (1), which houses the Cabinet, Minister's offices, and Bellamy's, site of parliamentary prandial privilege.

The neo-classical stone-built Parliament House (2), was completed in 1918, and replaces an earlier wooden building. When this building was restored in 1992–1995, 2000 tonnes of stone was required to match the original. This meant re-opening disused quarries to cut Kairuru marble from the Takaka Hills, and Coromandel granite from the Moehau Range.

During the restoration, the foundations of this building, and those of the Parliamentary Library (3), were rebuilt using modern techniques to resist earthquakes. Four hundred and seventeen rubber bearings, or base isolators, act as shock absorbers, allowing the foundations to move sideways by up to 30 cm each way. The buildings, cushioned from their foundations by these isolators, are subject to far less movement.

The oldest remaining building is the Gothic Parliamentary Library, which survived a 1907 fire owing to its brick construction. It was, unfortunately, badly damaged by fire during its refurbishment in 1992, but now stands exactly as it did in 1899, right

 200°

2   3   Map ref. [17]

down to the interior colour schemes. During the restoration, a fascinating discovery was made under the library's foundation stone. A brass container had been placed there on 13 April 1898 containing newspapers, coins, drawings and lists of Members of Parliament. A replacement time capsule of similar items was enclosed in the restored wall by the Speaker of the House, the Hon. Peter Tapsell.

Wellington at Dusk
The city lights at dusk against a dramatic sky are seen across Port Nicholson from Oriental Parade.

Civic Square, Wellington

Wellington's Civic Square is one of the finest public spaces in the world, created by the strategic location of new buildings to cut off vehicle access. Attractive new buildings, sympathetic renovations and complementary colour schemes are enhanced by imaginative open areas.

The Michael Fowler Centre (1) is named after the mayor under whose leadership Wellington City Council had the vision to build New Zealand's premier concert hall. Well-known architects Warren and Mahoney were commissioned to design the centre, drawing on their experience with Christchurch Town Hall. The result was an outstanding venue suitable for concerts, exhibitions, conventions and many smaller functions. Adjacent to the Michael Fowler Centre, and forming the other half of the Wellington Festival and Convention Centre, is the old Town Hall (2), an elegant neo-classical building serving the same variety of purposes.

The City Gallery (3), a fine building, displays contemporary New Zealand and overseas art. The nearby Capital Discovery Place is a hands-on science exhibition for children. A sweep of steps leads up to its roof, a plaza enlivened by sculptures, part of the City to Sea Link (4) which gives pedestrian access from Civic Square to the waterfront.

The buildings and spaces of Civic Square host many events, large and small, of the biennial International Festival of the Arts. For over three weeks in March, Wellington is graced by major artists from all over the world in a great celebration of music, dance, theatre and other art forms. Alongside the main festival is the more anarchic Fringe Festival in which 'alternative' and less established artists perform in smaller venues, or enliven the streets and squares of the city.

3   4   Map ref. [17]

The Michael Fowler Centre
The main auditorium, elegantly finished in native timbers, has been designed to produce superb acoustics and to afford a clear view of the stage from each of its 2500 seats. These features make it a popular venue for audiences and performers alike.

QUEEN CHARLOTTE SOUND, MARLBOROUGH

1

Always to islanders danger
Is what comes over the sea.
            Allen Curnow

The Marlborough Sounds were formed by the progressive downward movement of this section of the coast, lowering the intricate river valleys until they were inundated by the rising sea level. Queen Charlotte Sound (3) is one of the two main inlets of the intricate, island-studded coastline.

Captain Cook named Queen Charlotte Sound in 1770, after raising the Union Flag on Motuara Island and taking possession of the country for the King. In this claim he had exceeded his instructions, and the British Government were careful to exclude New Zealand from its list of territories for 70 years.

Cook made Ship Cove, near the mouth of the Sound, his base for his New Zealand explorations, spending 100 days here over a seven year period. At Ship Cove he found fresh water, easy fishing and green plants which could be brewed to ward off scurvy. He landed the country's first pair of sheep here, with a view to future provisions, but within three days they had eaten poisonous tutu and died. A similar experiment with sheep and goats, landed on Arapawa Island in 1777, was more successful in breeding terms, but led ultimately to widespread environmental damage on the island.

Picton (1) enjoys an incomparable setting at the head of Queen Charlotte Sound, with splendid views of the steep green coastline plunging into the still, sheltered waters. Freight ships and ferries (2) ply the Cook Strait between Picton and Wellington, and pleasure craft cruise the Sounds. Launch trips can be taken to explore the coves and inlets, to visit certain reserve islands, and to view the dolphins that frequent the outer waters.

250°

Map ref. [18]

Seals
Once hunted near to extinction in New Zealand for their fur, seals are now a common sight around the coast.

Centre of New Zealand, Nelson

1

For many New Zealand families, summer would not be complete without a holiday on or near the golden sands of Nelson.

On the north side of the Matai River in Nelson lies Botanical Hill, a 147 m prominence reached via the Botanical Reserve. At its summit is a trig point, marked by a stone, which was the point of origin for the original survey of the Nelson area. Local people also claim this, erroneously, as the geographical centre of New Zealand, and a large marker (1) was erected to this effect in 1968. In any case, the views over the city, coast and surrounding area are unrivalled.

Nelson's early days were marked by poverty and the near starvation of many of its inhabitants, with too many farm labourers and too few employers. Today, the city (2) and its port (3) have an air of prosperity, and levels of agricultural production are high. The arts and crafts thrive here, with pottery being a particular speciality owing to the availability of china clay. The equable climate, with mild winters and long hours of sunshine, adds to the prosperity and artistic atmosphere to create a city with an almost Mediterranean ambience.

Nelson vies with Christchurch for the honour of the title of New Zealand's first rugby union club. In fact, although Christchurch Football Club is older than that of Nelson, neither originally played rugby. The Nelson Football Club was formed in 1868 to play a hybrid of soccer and Australian Rules football. Rugby was introduced by Charles Munro, son of the Speaker of the House of Representatives, who had played at school in Britain. The first match was played on 14 May 1870 between Nelson Football Club and Nelson College at the Botanical Reserve. Thus the national sport began.

300°

2　　　　　　　　　　　3　　　　　　　　　　Map ref. [19]

Nile Street West
The street in which these fine wooden houses stand is named after one of Lord Nelson's famous battles; many other streets commemorate the English hero's exploits.

ABEL TASMAN NATIONAL PARK

1

It was one of those days so clear, so silent, so still, you almost feel the earth itself has stopped in astonishment at its own beauty.

Katherine Mansfield

Abel Tasman is New Zealand's smallest National Park, and one of its more recent, having been created in 1942 to commemorate the tercentenary of the first European sighting of the country by Dutch navigator Abel Tasman. Tasman's first anchorage was in Golden Bay near the Tata Islands, just off what is now the National Park. On arrival, the two Dutch vessels were inspected by two canoes of Maori warriors who blew a horn, the Dutch responding on a trumpet.

No further interaction occurred for several days, when a rowing boat crossing between the two ships was attacked. Four of the Dutch crew were killed before the attacking Maori withdrew under gunfire, without apparent loss of life. Tasman decided to leave 'as no friendship could be made with these people, no water nor refreshments could be obtained'. This discouraging encounter, at what Tasman christened Murderer's Bay, was the explorer's only attempt to land in the new country, a decision perhaps vindicated by the launching of a war party as he set sail.

The park was created too late to be a pristine wilderness; farming, milling and quarrying had modified the landscape significantly. However, where land was cleared by burning, the species invading after this devastation — bracken, gorse, manuka and radiata pine — are slowly being replaced by mature forest. Rainforest is regenerating in the lowlands, while beech predominates at higher levels.

Although easy walking tracks, such as the Loop Track (1), wind through the park, this is essentially a coastal area, best appreciated by sea or by air. Only thus can many of the idyllic coves and beaches, inaccessible by foot, be viewed. Ferries visit the most popular spots, such as Awaroa (2), which also has its own landing strip.

250°

Map ref. [20]

Awaroa captures the essence of Abel Tasman National Park: rivers running down to the sea between forested hills, golden sands, hidden coves and dramatic headlands.

Awaroa Lodge, in the heart of the park, provides an oasis of luxury for trampers and day trippers. Like most of the park, the lodge is not accessible by road, so staff must collect supplies by barge from the nearest road, a few kilometres up Awaroa Inlet.

Aerial View of Abel Tasman National Park
A flight with a local airline, such as Tasman Bay Aviation of Nelson, provides the most spectacular views of the coastline, such as the perfect crescent of Torrent Bay.

KAIKOURA

1

She was an enormous beast, lying quiescent in an area of dancing blue water...

Olaf Ruhen

Nestled in the northern face of the Kaikoura Peninsula (1), and overlooked by the Seaward Kaikoura Range (3), Kaikoura township (2) is a mecca for those who wish to see marine mammals in their natural environment. Whales, dolphins, seals, and a variety of other marine animals and sea birds, gather in abundance along this coast. Two factors create the conditions that allow so many creatures to thrive here.

The first factor is that Kaikoura is the meeting place for two ocean streams: subtropical waters moving southwards meet subantarctic waters travelling in the opposite direction. The colder waters are already rich in nutrients, but the meeting of the currents sweeps more nutrients up from the ocean floor into the lighter surface zone where they can be utilised by phytoplankton, innumerable floating single-celled plants that form the basis of the marine food chain. They are consumed by zooplankton, which in turn provide food for fish and other sea creatures. This abundance of food attracts larger predators such as sharks and marine mammals.

The second factor contributing to the variety of marine life on the Kaikoura Coast is geological. A submarine chasm, over 1000 m deep, extends out from the Hikurangi Trough to within 3 km of the coast at Kaikoura. This allows sperm whales, which feed in deep waters on giant squid and other large prey, to surface unusually close to shore.

The abundance of whales of many species so close to land brought first whaling ships, then a shore station to Kaikoura. However, as early as 1850, the decline in stocks made whaling uneconomic and the stations closed. The advent of motor

270°

2 3

Map ref. [21]

launches and harpoon guns led to a brief resurgence in the slaughter, but since the early years of this century the whales have gone unmolested in these waters.

In recent years, whales have again begun to play an economic role in the lives of the local people. Whale Watch™ Kaikoura Ltd, owned and operated by the Kai Tahu people, operates boat trips which offer visitors the opportunity of a close sighting of sperm whales and a variety of other wildlife.

The town's livelihood is now closely linked to this and other ecotourism operations, such as swimming with dolphins or seals.

Sperm Whale off Kaikoura
Only the male whales travel south to feed, the females preferring to stay in the warmer northern waters.

TRUMANS TRACK BEACH, PUNAKAIKI

1   2

This unnamed beach at the end of Trumans Track is as wild as any on the West Coast.

Trumans Track is a short walk through magnificent rainforest to the beach. The coastal fringe is typified by the beautiful Nikau palms which thrive because of the warm current from northeastern Australia which strikes the coast here.

The rocky foreshore at the northern end of the beach is an ideal haunt for crayfish, and at low tide fishermen perch precariously on the rocks trying to coax them from their holes (1).

Punakaiki, with its extraordinary stratified limestone formations, is part of New Zealand's newest national park, Paparoa, which stretches from the slopes of the Paparoa Range to the coast between Westport and Greymouth. Towering forested limestone cliffs line the rivers as they run down to the sea. In the narrow lowland coastal strip, the limestone has been shaped into cave systems by the plentiful streams. On the coast, the powerful Tasman Sea (2) has sculpted the cliffs and headlands into dramatic formations (3).

The road down the West Coast is a remarkable drive, with endless vistas of remote and rugged bays, and few other motorists to spoil the effect. The bays are complemented by steep, bush-clad hills, brimming with lush vegetation which thrives on the 5000 mm of rainfall that inundates the area annually.

305°

3   Map ref. [22]

Pancake Rocks, Dolomite Point
Pancake Rocks are best seen at high tide, when the waves surge noisily into the caverns below and are forced upwards through the blowholes.

Shantytown, Greymouth

1   2

Shantytown is a reminder of the West Coast's gold-mining history, in an area where many of the original gold-towns of the 1880s have long since crumbled into ruins.

The idea of Shantytown came from a meeting of railway and vintage car enthusiasts to discuss a means of preserving old gold-mining equipment and so create a tourist attraction. What is unique to Shantytown is that it was a true community project in which more than 10,000 hours' work were volunteered. Some of the buildings are originals which were shifted here, others are faithful replicas.

The interdenominational church (1) was originally built in the gold-mining settlement of No-Town in 1866. By 1922, No-Town was just that, a ghost town, and the church was shifted to Ngahere by horse and cart. It was donated to Shantytown in 1969 and its move there was the project of the West Coast Master Builders.

The railway station was built to plans supplied by New Zealand Railways (now Tranz Rail Ltd). Four steam trains are housed at Shantytown, including the locomotive *Kaitangata* (2), built in 1897 in Glasgow for the Kaitangata Coal Company. The engine follows an old sawmill tramline route to take visitors on a trip into the bush.

Various businesses typical of the time line the street, including Griffen and Smith's Beehive Store (3), established in 1865 in Greymouth. The neighbouring Golden Nugget Hotel was built with parts from many West Coast hotels. Robert Hannah, an Irish immigrant, set up a boot shop in Charleston, a booming gold-town 120 years ago and its name survives as a national chain of shoe shops (4). The Printing Works was built and equipped by the staff of the *Greymouth Evening Star*, and contains a press made in 1837 and in use in Napier until the 1950s.

290°

3 4 Map ref. [23]

Jeweller's shop, Shantytown

This celebration of the watchmaker's and jeweller's craft is a tribute to Barney Sutherland, MBE, a jeweller from Greymouth who provided the inspiration for the founding of Shantytown.

Canterbury Plains

1

Tena ko te toa mahi kai e kore e paheke.
The warrior who works hard to grow food will not fail.

Canterbury has the most contrasting landscapes of any region in New Zealand, being home to the highest mountains, including the Mount Hutt Range (2), and the widest area of flat land in the country. The Canterbury Plains were formed by gravel produced by erosion and brought down by the rivers from the Southern Alps and their foothills. The slope of the land becomes ever more gradual as it nears the coast, until it levels out entirely.

Canterbury is renowned for its agricultural production, particularly sheep but also cattle, cereals and fruit. The flat tract of land which forms the Plains is particularly well suited to mechanisation and, hence, cereal growing. Wheat is the main cereal crop, but in this photograph the harvest of black oats is under way.

Harvest is the culmination of a year's work for Canterbury farmer Don Baxter (1), seen here in his 12 hectare paddock checking the moisture content of the grain with the Gorman brothers, contracted to harvest the crop.

Contracting out the harvest is commonplace because of the high capital cost of machinery, but the farmer and contractor need to agree on the right moment, when not only the weather but also the moisture content of the crop is right. Fortunately, the area is renowned for long, hot summers which speed the ripening of the grain and make harvesting easier. The region is also the driest in the country, receiving only 750 mm of rain a year, compared to 5000 mm in the adjacent West Coast.

The patchwork effect of the fields and paddocks, bordered by hedges and wind breaks, makes the Plains reminiscent of the East Anglia region of England. Indeed, the region was named after an English city, home of the highest see of the Anglican Church, since this area was settled primarily by members of the Church of England.

265°

2

Map ref. [24]

Canterbury Skies
The flatness of the Canterbury Plains make the skies here seem more expansive than in other parts of the country, with dramatic cloud formations illuminated by the evening sun.

CATHEDRAL SQUARE, CHRISTCHURCH

1

Cathedral Square is a reminder that it was the dream of the founders of Christchurch that the city be a 'transplanted English community, possessing English ideals and English institutions…'

Christchurch Cathedral (1) was designed by B.W. Mountfort, who was also responsible for many other Gothic Revival buildings in the city. Work began in 1864, but suffered several setbacks because of adverse economic conditions. The nave was consecrated in 1881 but, as with the ancient cathedrals of Europe, additions have been made right up to the present day. The most recent development is the Cathedral Visitors Centre, opened by the Queen in 1995, which provides information, and houses a café.

Many people expound their views at Speaker's Corner outside the cathedral, but none so eccentric as the Wizard who, like the cathedral, is a Christchurch institution and tourist attraction.

The foundation stone of the simple Italianate Chief Post Office building (2) was laid in 1877. The transfer of the post office to Cathedral Square hastened the demise of the original marketplace (which later became Victoria Square) as the civic and commercial heart of the city. Plaques on the building commemorate the establishment in 1862 of the Lyttelton–Christchurch telegraph line, the first government telegraph service in New Zealand and, in 1881, the first telephone exchange in the country.

The Regent Theatre (3) was originally designed by S. and A.E. Luttrell as the Royal Exchange Building, but changed its use and its name in 1929 when it became a cinema. Its first auditorium had impressive Spanish-style decor, with a projection of a starry night sky on the ceiling.

Four Ships Court, between the post office and the Regent Theatre, contains pavement plaques commemorating each of the first four ships that carried the founding

colonists to the city site in 1850. There is also a plaque in memory of the 'pre-Adamite' settlers, a small group of immigrants who farmed the Canterbury Plains from 1843.

A statue in the square commemorates John Robert Godley, founder of Christchurch in 1850 and after whose Oxford college the city is named.

Christchurch Cathedral
The 63 m spire of the cathedral has been damaged three times in earthquakes: the tip of the spire is now copper, following the loss of part of the stone structure in 1901.

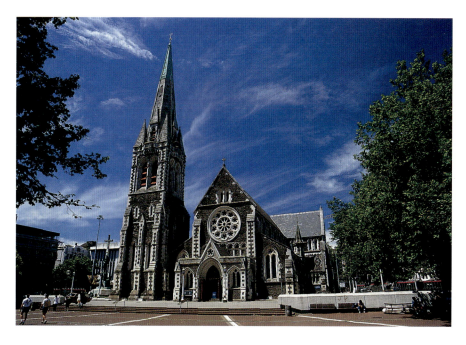

CHRIST'S COLLEGE, CHRISTCHURCH

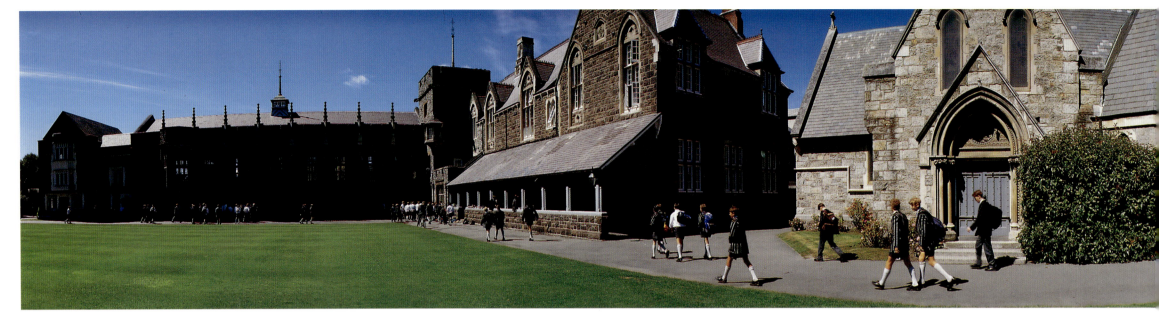

1

Christ's College was intended to 'resemble as nearly as possible the English Public Schools', and, by its 'massive strength, stability and simplicity', give a lesson to its pupils.

Under the Canterbury Settlement scheme, one third of all revenue from land sales was to be set aside for religion and education.

Thus, Christ's College was one of the first institutions in Christchurch, planned in England even before the departure of the ships which brought the Canterbury Pilgrims to found their Anglican settlement.

The appointed headmaster, the Reverend Henry Jacobs, sailed on *Sir George Seymour*, arriving on 18 December 1850 and starting his school of five pupils at the Lyttelton Immigration Barracks the following year. The school occupied another temporary site until, after a delay of several years, the present land had been granted and the first building erected in 1857.

The Headmaster's House, the wooden building to which the College moved, was burned to the ground ten years later, leaving the stone-built Big School (2) (1863) to lay claim to being the oldest educational building in New Zealand.

The building which accommodates Harper and Julius Dayboy Houses (1) was designed by B.W. Mountfort, although a number of architects contributed to the school project. One of Mountfort's earliest buildings, a church at Lyttelton, had to be demolished before it collapsed. Not surprisingly, this damaged his reputation for some time and one of the posts he took during this period was that of drawing master at Christ's College. Christchurch is fortunate that he was able eventually to resurrect his architectural career and leave a legacy of fine neo-Gothic buildings.

295°

2   Map ref. [25]

Over the years, the College has developed a fine precinct of buildings of different ages but of blending styles, set around an open grassy quadrangle. The 10 acre site was granted out of the Government Domain which developed into the Botanical Gardens and Hagley Park, so despite its city centre setting, the College is situated in a green haven.

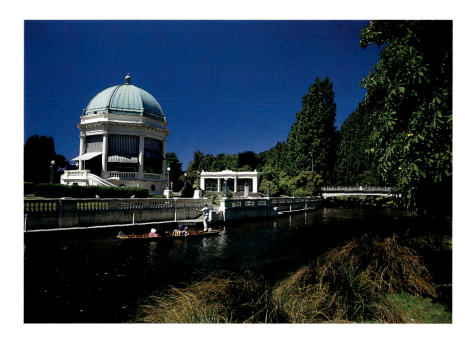

Punting on the Avon River
Punts, complete with suitably attired boatman, float tourists along the willow-lined river, adding to the English air of the city.

77

WORCESTER BOULEVARD, CHRISTCHURCH

1 2

The Arts Centre of Christchurch on Worcester Boulevard is another fine example of the city reclaiming its past with flair and ensuring that it continues to enrich the present.

The Arts Centre occupies the original buildings of the University of Canterbury. Canterbury College, as it was first known, was founded in 1873, but the first permanent building on this site, the clock tower (2) designed by B.W. Mountfort, was not completed until 1877. The Great Hall (3) was opened on Diploma Day in 1882.

The buildings on the site were built over a period of 50 years, but achieve a remarkable unity because of Samuel Hurst Seager's vision of two quadrangles with the buildings linked by arcades, giving the impression of medieval cloisters. The University of Canterbury had long outgrown this site by 1975 when it completed its move to the new campus at Ilam.

The most notable graduate (in 1894) of Canterbury College was Ernest (Lord) Rutherford, 'the father of the atom'. During his time here, he conducted experiments in very high frequency magnetisation of iron. The basement den in which some of this work was undertaken has been restored, and is open to the public.

Canterbury College also has the distinction of being the first in the British Empire to admit women to its classes, the first woman honours graduate being Helen Connon (MA, 1881).

The Arts Centre is the largest in New Zealand, and within its old walls can be found shops, cafés, craftspeople, artists, musicians, a theatre, a cinema, and much more. At the weekend the bustle increases with an open air craft market.

Canterbury Museum (5), another of Mountfort's designs, was opened in 1870 under the directorship of Sir Julius von Haast. Haast was a major figure in the

exploration of the South Island, his geological surveys leading to the opening of routes between Canterbury and Westland. He was also Professor of Geology at Canterbury College.

In 1995, the city saw the return of its trams after an absence of more than 40 years. Beautifully restored old trams now loop around the most scenic areas of the city centre, carrying tourists and residents alike. Tram No. 11 — *The Boxcar* — has been specially decorated for the city's annual flower festival (4) and is seen here nearing the city's town crier (1), who hasn't dressed up for the occasion.

New Regent Street
When New Regent Street was built in the Depression, only three tenants could be found for these Spanish Mission-style shops, whereas now it is a thriving centre of cafés and specialist retailers.

LYTTELTON HARBOUR, BANKS PENINSULA

Major ports rarely exist in an attractive setting without destroying that beauty. Lyttelton, far from dominating the landscape, is dwarfed by the surrounding Port Hills and harbour.

Lyttelton Harbour, like Akaroa Harbour, is the submerged crater of one of the two volcanoes that formed Banks Peninsula. Its first European discoverer was Captain C. Chase of the sealer *Pegasus* in 1810. It was named Port Cooper, but this was changed in 1848 to Port Victoria, then to Lyttelton after Lord Lyttelton, a supporter of Canterbury settlement.

Lyttelton was chosen as the port for the Canterbury settlement in 1848 by Captain Joseph Thomas, surveyor for the Canterbury Association. Development began in advance of the arrival of the first four ships carrying 800 settlers. The 'Canterbury Pilgrims' crossed the ridge of the Port Hills surrounding the harbour and established themselves at what is now Christchurch.

The Port Hills were a problem until the road around the coast to Sumner and over the Evans Pass was completed in 1857. A railway tunnel through the hills was opened in 1867, but a road tunnel did not follow until 1964.

Today, more than 1300 vessels call at the port each year. It is the main port for the South Island and thus vital to the local and regional economy.

Ripa Island (2) was the site of a Maori pa destroyed during tribal strife in 1821. It was later a European fort.

Quail Island (3) was used as a quarantine station for the dogs, ponies and mules used by Captain R.F. Scott and Sir Ernest Shackleton on their Antarctic expeditions.

The Lyttelton timeball station (4) was constructed in 1876, on a site visible to all ships in the harbour, to house a 'timeball'. The zinc ball was dropped down its mast at exactly one o'clock Greenwich Mean Time each day. This allowed sea captains to

325°

2   3   Map ref. [26]

reset their chronometers and so make accurate calculations of longitude by comparing Greenwich time with local time. Greenwich time was telegraphed to the timeball station from the observatory in Wellington.

Lyttelton Timeball Station
The now obsolete timeball station, superseded by technology.

AKAROA, BANKS PENINSULA

1

Akaroa is unique in New Zealand as the only township founded by French settlers, and it retains its Gallic charm. The colonists landed in French Bay (2).

Akaroa Harbour (1) is a long narrow inlet on the south side of the Banks Peninsula. The peninsula was formed following the eruption of two volcanoes, the craters of which became Akaroa and Lyttelton Harbours.

The first inhabitants of the area were moa hunters, who were succeeded by Ngati Mamoe, then Ngai Tahu from the north. The pa at Onawe Peninsula in Akaroa Harbour was overwhelmed in 1831 during a musket-reinforced raid by the Ngati Toa chief Te Rauparaha.

The area was thus thinly populated in 1838 when a French whaling captain, Jean Langlois, saw the sheltered harbour as having potential for settlement and for shipping. He made a payment to local Maori chiefs to purchase land, then returned to France to organise the first shipload of colonists under the auspices of the Nanto-Bordelaise Company. On 19 February 1840, a French naval ship, *L'Aube*, was dispatched in advance of the *Comte de Paris* which carried Langlois and the emigrants. When the captain of *L'Aube*, Charles Lavaud, reached the Bay of Islands on 11 July 1840, he learned that the Treaty of Waitangi had already established British sovereignty over the whole of New Zealand. The French settlement was allowed to proceed unhindered, but under British jurisdiction, and British settlers joined the community.

Today there are still descendants of the original settlers in the town. Many of the streets have French names and some of the older buildings show French touches in their architecture.

245°

2 Map ref. [26]

Langlois-Eteneveaux Cottage
This house, partly prefabricated in France around 1846, now forms part of Akaroa Museum.

Lake Heron

1

Kotahi te rerenga o te kotuku rerenga-tahi.
Once is the flight of the rare kotuku.

With the Taylor Range (1) as a backdrop, Lake Heron sits as a pool of crystal clear water, popular with fishermen for its rainbow trout and land-locked salmon. A wildlife refuge, it is home to a variety of birds, including the rare crested grebe.

Lake Heron was first discovered by Europeans in 1857 when T.H. Potts explored the area looking for suitable sheep runs with F.P.G. Leach and H. Phillips. Potts, an observant naturalist, named the lake from 'seeing so many white herons gently sailing over its surface or standing motionless on its stony beach'. During their foray the men accidentally set fire to the tussock while cooking and had to retreat to the bed of the Cameron River, where they spent the night. As a result of the expedition, Leach decided to apply for the land around Lake Heron, while Potts preferred the land around the lake they had named Clear Water. As well as being a pioneer runholder, Potts was a writer and diarist whose work gave a graphic account of the lives of the early Canterbury settlers.

One of the runs around Lake Heron was held briefly by the novelist Samuel Butler, who came to New Zealand in 1860 with £4,000, on a mission to double his money as quickly as possible by sheepfarming. He bought a number of leases to the

210°

Map ref. [27]

northeast of Lake Heron, naming his station Mesopotamia, and also owned Stronecruthie, now known as Erewhon Station. A series of articles for the Christchurch *Press* expressed views which were later published in his novel *Erewhon,* a satirical attack on Darwinism and conventional religion. Perhaps spurred on by the shortage of people with whom he could discuss the Arts, Butler achieved his financial goal in just four years, and returned to England where he devoted himself to writing.

Lake Hayes
Lake Hayes is another beautiful South Island lake, its tranquillity sometimes passed over for the grandeur of Lake Wakatipu.

Franz Josef Glacier

1 2

The frozen landscape of the Franz Josef Glacier, with its turquoise and blue hues, ice caves and ice pinnacles, is one of the most dramatic views in New Zealand.

Emerging between the Fritz Range (1) and the Baird Range (3), Franz Josef Glacier, along with its neighbour, Fox Glacier, is unique in descending to a very low altitude in a temperate zone. The glacier descends for 12 km from the main divide of the Southern Alps to about 300 m above sea level at its terminal face, where the Waiho River emerges. The glacier advances or retreats depending on whether the rate of accumulation of snow or the rate of melting is greater. It was in advance between 1992 and 1995.

Ice moves down the glacier at a very fast rate — a 5 m advance in one day has been recorded at the icefall (4), the steepest slope, although 1 m is more usual. The reason this glacier is so dramatic is threefold: the high snowfall in these mountains, the wide area from which ice pushes into the valley, and the steep gradient of the glacier.

The fast movement of Franz Josef Glacier means that the surface features change rapidly, with new ice caves (2) and crevasses opening up frequently. These features will last only a few weeks before they are transformed.

The glacier was sighted from the sea by Abel Tasman in 1642 and by James Cook in 1770. It was named after the emperor of the Austro-Hungarian Empire, Franz Josef, by the explorer and geologist Sir Julius von Haast in 1865.

280°

3   4   Map ref. [28]

Franz Josef Glacier from the Air
A trip to the glacier by helicopter adds excitement and an interesting perspective to your visit.

Mount Cook

1

2

...hills and more hills, deep valleys with caves and twisting rivers, and mountains white with winter in the distance.

Maurice Shadbolt

At 3764 m, Mount Cook, or Aorangi (cloud-piercer) (2), is the highest mountain in New Zealand, forming the dramatic centrepiece of a national park famous for its high peaks. The three peaks of Mount Cook are permanently mantled in snow, a stark contrast to the bare rock of its immense base. Other notable peaks seen here include Mount Sefton (1), 3157 m, and Mount Wakefield (3), 2050 m, below which the Hooker River (4) meanders. Mount Cook was named after Captain James Cook, though he never saw this magnificent mountain.

New Zealand's highest peak was first conquered by three New Zealanders — Fyfe, Graham and Clarke — in response to an attempt by an Englishman and an Italian. The New Zealanders reached the summit on Christmas Day 1894 and, although many others have since climbed Mount Cook, no one else followed their route until 61 years later, in the one hundredth ascent.

In December 1991, an substantial part of the east face of Mount Cook was brought down in a massive avalanche, which dislodged 14 million cubic metres of rock and forged a path 3 km wide and 7 km long down to the Tasman Glacier. Geoff Wyatt, who climbed that route the day before, became the last person to climb the old east face before it was gone forever. He was also the last mountaineer to climb to the previous height of Mount Cook, since it was left 10 m shorter by the fall.

The mountain is a focal point of climbing in New Zealand, with mountaineers from all over the world coming to scale its peak. The conqueror of Mount Everest, Sir Edmund Hillary, used Mount Cook as a training ground for his ascent of the world's highest peak in 1953.

335°

3　　　　　　　　　　　　　　　　　　　　　　　　4　　　　　　　　　　　　　　　　　　　　　5　　　　　　Map ref. [29]

Mount Cook village (5) exists to service the National Park and its visitors. Its most famous building is the Hermitage Hotel, founded in 1884, when tourists had to travel for days to reach it. The first building was destroyed in 1813 in a flash flood, and the second was burned to the ground in 1957. It is to be hoped that the current building, award winning in its time, survives longer.

Mount Cook from the Tasman Valley
The contrast between the mountain and the river flat is stark, the browns and greys of the valley setting off the snowy heights to good effect.

Tasman Glacier

1   2   3

Cutting across Mount Cook National Park is the 27 km Tasman Glacier, the longest in New Zealand and one of the longest in the world in a temperate zone.

The ice of the Tasman Glacier is 600 m deep in places, constantly topped up by its two tributary glaciers, the Ball and the Hochstetter, which feed in snow from the Grand Plateau on the eastern flank of Mount Cook (2) and from Mount Tasman. For its last few kilometres, the glacier is almost horizontal and covered by the mass of debris it carried down the mountain, so it appears to be a long, grey river of ground rock. Its movement of 60 cm a day not only grinds away the rocky mountainside, but also creates an ever changing landscape of crevasses and seracs in its upper reaches.

As with other glaciers around the world, the Tasman is in a period of retreat. Prior to 13,000 years ago, the Tasman formed part of a giant glacier system which occupied much of the Mackenzie Basin, the Tasman itself reaching another 50 km to the end of what is now Lake Pukaki. A loop of moraine developed, allowing the lake to form from meltwater. Even 100 years ago, visitors had to climb about 10 m up a moraine wall to reach the glacier, whereas today the ice lies 100 m below that spot.

The glacier was the first place in the world that a ski plane was used. The plane, invented in 1955 by Harry Wigley (later Sir Henry) of the Mount Cook Line, landed on the Tasman Glacier, witnessed by Sir Edmund Hillary. The retractable skis, which had formica runners, are on display at Mount Cook airport along with a small display of press cuttings illustrating the pioneering history of the company.

The easiest way to experience the glacier is still by ski plane, which transports

360°

4 5 Map ref. [30]

sightseers, mountaineers and skiers to sites such as the Upper Neve (4). For the skiers, the reward is two 12 km runs, led by experienced guides, taking in views of ice falls, crevasses, ice caves, and the surrounding peaks, including Mount Darwin (1), the Minarets (3) and the Tasman Saddle (5).

Tasman Valley from the Air
The Tasman River emerges from the terminal lake and flows through the wide gravel beds of the valley left by the retreating Tasman Glacier.

Ailsa Pass, Liebig Range

1 2 3

…the Southern Alps were our true landmark, dividing, ordering, surveying, illuminating our lives.

Janet Frame

The Southern Alps were formed by the upward thrust of the earth's crust created by the collision of the Pacific and Indian-Australian plates. The mountains of the Liebig Range and others in the Mount Cook National Park are still being forced upward at a rate of 5–10 mm per year, but this is counteracted by the forces of erosion. The rock of these mountains is highly susceptible to erosion, as is evidenced by the bare rock and scree slopes seen in the Ailsa Pass rock formation (5).

Mount Malte Brun (1) was first climbed in 1893 by a 24-year-old plumber named Tom Fyfe. Fyfe descended a great deal faster than he had intended, when an avalanche of rocks started above him. Fyfe has passed into legend with his skillful descent, using his ice axe as a third body support and glissading down a snowy gully ahead of the rocks.

Other notable peaks seen in this panorama include Mount Tamaki (2443 m) (2), Mount Lucia (2591 m) (3), and the Gammock Range (4).

Much of the National Park can be reached only on foot, but some remote areas provide landing sites for helicopters, such as those flown by the Mount Cook Airline. The history of the Mount Cook Group of companies is an interesting one, intimately bound up with the story of tourism in New Zealand.

At the beginning of the century, the company of Wigley & Thornley was operating steam traction engines to haul wool bales out of the Mackenzie Country. One of the partners, Rodolph Wigley, was fascinated by the new vistas opened up by the internal combustion engine, and in 1906 purchased a 6 hp De Dion car. In February of that year, he and a friend set out in two cars to drive from Fairlie to the Hermitage Hotel

330°

4 5 Map ref. [31]

below Mount Cook, arriving at 4 a.m. This was the first journey to Mount Cook by motor vehicle and by November 1906, Wigley had started a scheduled service that was to form the nucleus of the well-known travel company.

Mountain Lake
In Mount Cook National Park small lakes take on a vivid turquoise hue amidst the surrounding grey rock.

The Mackenzie Country

South into the high barren hills, the anchored remote land, the intense country of shades and storms and snows and sun...crystals and desert.

Keri Hulme

Horses are a traditional part of life in the Mackenzie Country, and are a familiar sight in this rugged sheep country. Horse trekking is a popular activity, such as this trek led by Gaye Simpson (1) at Mount John Station at Lake Tekapo.

Legend goes that the bare, brown high country that now bears his name was discovered by Scottish drover James McKenzie, who applied for a run in Otago then attempted to stock it with sheep stolen from the Levels Station at Timaru. He was certainly apprehended in 1855 near Mackenzie Pass in charge of 1000 stolen sheep by the Levels overseer and two Maori shepherds from the station. McKenzie escaped and made his way to Lyttelton where he might have escaped from Canterbury by ship, had he not been captured by a police sergeant while hiding in a loft.

During his trial, he refused to speak and pretended not to understand what was going on. The story goes that his dog, Friday, was brought into the courtroom and rushed to her master, thus confirming his identity, despite his being 'mute of malice'. McKenzie was sentenced to five years' imprisonment.

Recent research suggests a possible miscarriage of justice, and subsequent embellishments of the facts by those involved at the time. The story that McKenzie told to his gaoler after his trial was that he had been hired by one James Mossman to help him drive the sheep to Otago, and had been paid £20 for the job, a sum which was found on him at his committal. Mossman, he said, had fled before the pursuers arrived, which may have been borne out by the overseer's evidence that he had followed the footprints of at least two men with the sheep. No application in McKenzie's name for a run has been found.

250°

1   Map ref. [32]

McKenzie's gaoler pressed for a pardon, which the Superintendent of Canterbury forwarded to the Governor with the words, 'I am inclined to believe his story'. One could speculate that the gaoler was keen to be rid of the responsibility for a man who kept escaping, but in any case an unconditional pardon was granted.

The dog's story also has a happy end, despite a myth that she was hung or shot. She is believed to have become a favourite of George Rhodes, owner of the stolen sheep, although presumably she had been trained to respond to commands in Gaelic, the only language in which her former master was fluent.

Hay Bales in Summer
Hay is produced in summer in the Mackenzie to see the livestock through the harsh high country winter.

Church of the Good Shepherd, Lake Tekapo

This church was designed to 'give the impression of quiet strength and simplicity' which symbolized the runholders of the Mackenzie Country.

The Church of the Good Shepherd (2) is dedicated to 'the Glory of God and as a memorial to the pioneers of the Mackenzie Country'. It was built in 1935, using stones gathered within a 5 mile radius and carried by hand to the construction site. The stones were left unhewn and the land around the church was left undisturbed, strewn with boulders and matagouri bushes. The resulting church reflects the ruggedness of the landscape and the people, underpinned by tranquillity.

The fittings of oak are a reminder of the pioneers' British origins, and were donated by their descendants. The altar is made from a single block of Oamaru stone, carved by well-known sculptor F.G. Gurnsey. Gurnsey also carved the font, dedicated to 'all shepherds and station hands', decorating it with the flora and fauna of the high country. As in a number of other New Zealand churches, the east window behind the altar is of plate glass. The view out over the lake to the Sibbald Range (1) beyond is a constant reminder of the work of the Creator.

A little further along the lake front from the church stands another memorial, a statue of a sheepdog sculpted by a local woman. This is a tribute to the work of these animals, without which the stocking of the Mackenzie Country would not have been possible.

210°

1 2 Map ref. [33]

Lake Tekapo
Lake Tekapo is fed by glacial waters, which bring down rock flour, a fine powder ground from the mountains by the action of ice. The suspended particles give the lake its famous pale turquoise colour and opacity.

THAMES STREET, OAMARU

1   2

The splendid Victorian architecture of Oamaru, constructed of the local limestone, testifies that this has always been a prosperous town full of civic pride.

Oamaru was intended to be a major port for the South Island, but although this was never a great commercial success the town did boom during the general prosperity of the gold rush, and became the service centre for the farms and estates of the interior. This would not have been enough to account for the large number of substantial historic buildings in the town, had it not been for the local stone.

Oamaru stone is an almost pure limestone found in thick horizontal beds with no vertical joints. When first quarried, it is soft enough to be cut with a circular saw, hardening to become very weather-resistant. This makes it a convenient, permanent and relatively cheap building material.

While the nearby Tyne and Harbour Streets were the first to be developed, being nearer the port, as the town expanded Thames Street became the home of even grander buildings. The Last Post pub occupies Oamaru's oldest surviving public building, the first post office (1) built in 1864. It was eclipsed by the Forrester and Lemon designed second post office (2), built next door in 1884, which now houses Waitaki District Council. Across the road stands the National Bank (3), which took over the Bank of Otago which this building, built in 1871, originally housed. The classical styling complements that of the adjacent Bank of New South Wales (4) — now the Forrester Gallery. Both were the work of prominent Dunedin architect R.A. Lawson, although they differ markedly from the Gothic Revival style in which he worked in that city.

245°

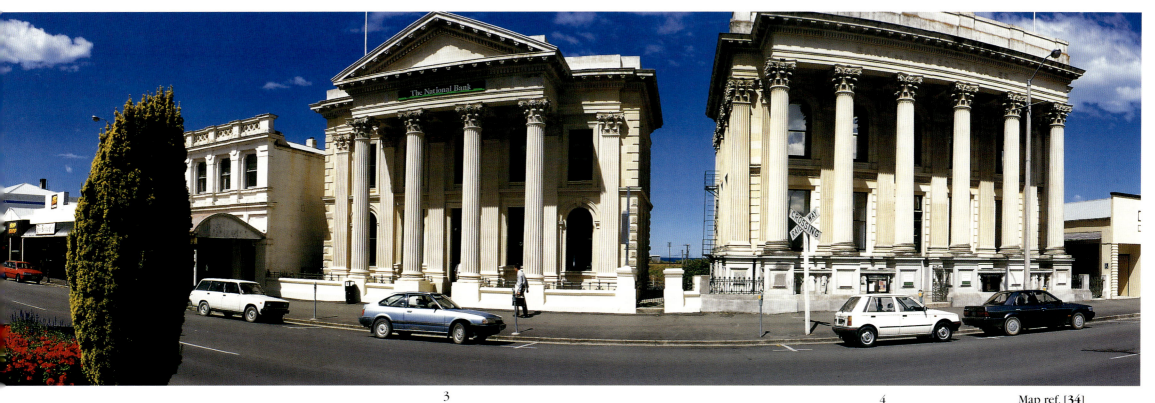

3 4 Map ref. [34]

Waitaki Boys High School, Oamaru
The first part of the school was built in 1883, with additions in 1905 and 1912 designed by Forrester and Lemon, the local practice which dominated architecture in the town for several decades.

Moeraki Boulders, Hampden Beach

1

Like long abandoned eggs of some huge, pre-historic creature, or mystical symbols from an alien civilisation, these boulders lie forlornly on the sands between Moeraki and Hampden.

The Ngai Tahu tribe describe the boulders as the food baskets and water storage gourds washed ashore after the wreck of the great canoe Arai-te-uru at nearby Shag Point. The canoe and its passengers give the names to various topographical features in the area. Today, the cooking connection is maintained in the café and visitor centre (1), designed to reflect the spherical nature of the boulders.

The geological explanation of the origin of these gigantic stones is more prosaic. The process by which they formed began 60 million years ago in the seabed. Within a homogeneous layer of wet sediment, the mineral calcite gradually migrated to, and crystallised around, a nucleus of organic matter. In this way, it is estimated that small 'concretions' took about 120,000 years to form, while large ones took appproximately 4 million years.

Next, the concretions began to dry out, and shrinkage cracks radiated out from the centre. The cracks filled up with two types of calcite, in the form of brown and yellow crystals. By this time, this area of the seabed had risen up to form part of the coastal belt of the newly formed New Zealand landmass, eventually becoming the eroded cliffs seen today.

The boulders are embedded in the soft mudstone cliff and are released on to the beach as the sea erodes the cliff face. As the boulder is exposed to the elements on the beach (2), the outer layer is gradually eroded away, revealing the calcite filled veins radiating from its centre. Eventually, the boulder fragments along these lines and breaks up (3).

250°

2   3   Map ref. [35]

Birth of a Boulder
Stone born of stone, with a gestation period that exceeds man's presence on this planet.

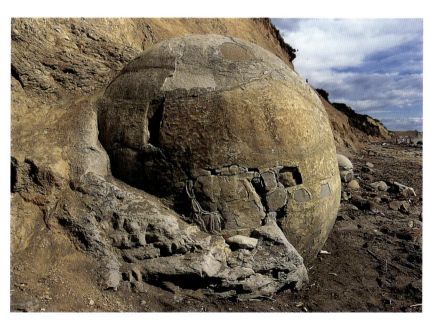

Larnach Castle, Otago Peninsula

1

Sitting proudly on the Otago Peninsula overlooking Dunedin, the Harbour and the open coast, Larnach Castle (2) is one man's dream of a Highland stronghold.

Larnach Castle, originally known as The Camp, was designed by R.A. Lawson, the architect of a number of public buildings in Dunedin, for William Larnach. The cost of the work — £125,000 — was enormous for its time (1871), and made possible only by the £85,000 fortune of Larnach's first wife, Eliza de Guise. Materials for the building came from all over the world: New Zealand kauri and Oamaru stone, Italian marble and glass, English ceramic tiles, American Douglas fir, and so on. All these had to be punted across the harbour from Port Chalmers and dragged up the hill by ox-drawn sleds.

An unusual feature of the castle was the lighting system. Horse manure was drained into a small building behind the castle and there made into methane gas. This was pumped up to the castle using a foot pump and supplied to the chandeliers through lead pipes.

Lanarch Castle features a bandstand (1) and a ballroom (3), which today serves as a cafeteria, dispensing coffee and cakes to visitors from around the world.

William Larnach came to Dunedin from New South Wales to manage the Bank of Otago, later being involved in a number of businesses and entering Parliament. Historically, his most interesting business venture was as managing director of the New Zealand Refrigeration Company which in 1882 launched the world's first refrigerated vessel, carrying meat and butter.

In 1876 he was elected Member of Parliament for Dunedin, later taking a number

250°

Map ref. [36]

of ministerial offices, including Mines, the Colonial Treasury, and Public Works and Railways. Larnach had three wives, the first two of whom were half-sisters. When his first wife died, Larnach put a private bill through Parliament to change the law, allowing him to marry his sister-in-law.

Larnach's career ended in tragedy when he took his own life in Parliament House in 1898 following a scandal.

The Master Bedroom
This room at Larnach Castle contains an original kauri bed with bird's eye kauri panels. Large windows on three sides of the room give it commanding views over the Otago Peninsula.

OLVESTON, DUNEDIN

1

2

The marvellous Jacobean-style architecture and lavish furnishings of Olveston were the unique gift of Dorothy Theomin to the city of Dunedin. Today, over 40,000 visitors a year enjoy the atmosphere of this gracious Edwardian mansion.

Olveston was designed by London architect Sir Ernest George, and built between 1904 and 1906 for businessman Edward Theomin and his wife, Marie. This is George's only known house in the southern hemisphere, and reflects his interest in Jacobean architecture combined with attention to detail in the smallest of internal fittings. The house is graced with warm wooden panelling, grand staircases, stained glass windows, focal fireplaces, and elegant brass door plates, light fittings and switches. It was equipped from the start with all modern conveniences such as electric light, central heating, an in-house telephone system and a goods lift.

The house is more than a monument to the architect's skill, it is a family treasure-house. Edward and Marie Theomin were avid collectors of fine art, a tradition followed by their daughter, Dorothy, who inherited the house. Much of the Japanese and Chinese collection is housed in the Billiard Room, seen here.

The floor of the Billiard Room is strengthened with steel girders to support the two tonne table (2). The room is equipped with a scoreboard cabinet with the accessories for not only billiards but also a number of other table games. Windows in the ceiling provide good light in the daytime, and extra ventilation when necessary. A raised couch (1) permits comfortable viewing of games in progress.

A small annexe, the Card Room (3), provides a comfortable corner for games or gossip. Its exotic Persian furnishings provide a contrast to the Englishness of the rest of the house. The 'Juliet Window' in this room overlooks the Great Hall, allowing communication between guests in different parts of the house.

235°

3   Map ref. [37]

University of Otago, Dunedin
Dunedin has the country's oldest and most illustrious university, founded in 1869. The original university building, with its splendid clocktower, was designed by Maxwell Bury in the Gothic Revival style, which was reflected in subsequent campus buildings.

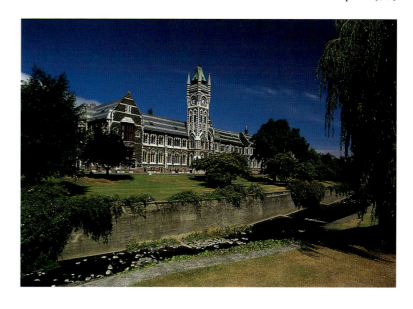

Purakaunui Falls, Catlins

We first arrived at the Purakaunui Falls in the pouring rain, the sound of water was everywhere and you could almost hear the vegetation growing.

The Purakaunui Falls Reserve is 500 hectares of native bush which has been protected since 1905. A short walk through mixed podocarp and beech forest leads to where the Purakaunui River cascades down 20 m in a three-tiered waterfall (1). The track leads to the head of the falls then descends to a lower viewing platform (2) from where this photograph was taken.

The beauty of the location is not reflected in its placename. Purakaunui means 'Big Stack of Firewood', a name referring to the bodies of slain Maori warriors piled up ready for cooking.

The Reserve is in the Catlins district, where rolling hill country drops down to a spectacular and remote coastline. As well as Purakaunui Falls, the twisting, tortuous Southern Scenic Drive offers many other interesting stops, such as Porpoise Bay, where you may see Hectors dolphins, and Curio Bay, where the sea ebbs to reveal fossils at low tide.

The area was once inhabited by moa hunters, followed by whalers and then loggers. Small farms grew up on the cleared land, but did not prosper and were absorbed into larger properties. Once again, the population of the area dwindled, so that today the largest settlement, Owaka, about 15 km away, has only a few hundred residents. The low population adds to the attraction of this area of fascinating native flora and fauna.

350°

Map ref. [38]

Purakaunui Stream
This whole area is so verdant and alive. Don't miss the plant information plaques beside the footpath which follows the course of the stream to the falls.

TAIERI GORGE RAILWAY, CENTRAL OTAGO

1

The Taieri Gorge route from Dunedin to Middlemarch in Central Otago is one of the great railway journeys of the world, crossing tributary creeks on viaducts and plunging into tunnels through rocky outcrops, with another breathtaking view at every bend.

The Taieri Gorge Railway is a substantial remnant of the now defunct Otago Central Railway, which ran from Wingatui Junction near Dunedin to Cromwell, 235 km away. By the 1870s, the Central Otago goldrush was over and greater access to markets was needed to allow further development of Dunedin's hinterland. Towns such as Cromwell, Alexandra and Clyde could only be reached by a bone-shaking two day road journey, while goods loaded on wagons travelled at a mere 30 km per day. It is not surprising, therefore, that in 1871, representatives of Central Otago began to petition for a railway line in the area.

It was not until 1877 that a route was chosen which opened up the greatest area of Crown lands and presented the fewest engineering difficulties. Construction began two years later, but was almost immediately hit by the economic depression of the 1880s. It took ten years to construct the first 27 km to Hindon in the middle of the gorge, but the 38 km to Middlemarch was finished in just two years. The line through to Cromwell, however, was not completed until 1921, 50 years after the idea of a railway to serve Central Otago was first mooted.

In December 1989 the Minister of Railways announced that the line would be closed at the end of April 1990. The Mayor of Dunedin quickly responded that the city would buy the line as far as Middlemarch, if the community could raise $1 million for the project. There was considerable support for this idea, as the line had long been a focal point for railway enthusiasts, and special sightseeing excursions had been running for years. By July 1990, $1.2 million had been raised and 60 km of

2

3   Map ref. [39]

line plus locomotives and carriages were purchased. The train, the *Taieri Gorge Limited* (1), which comprises a mixture of refurbished 1920s carriages and specially designed ones built in Dunedin, runs regular four-hour excursions through the gorge, traversing structures such as the Deep Stream Viaduct (2), which has a span of 81 m, and bridges Deep Stream Gully (3), 16 m below.

Dunedin Railway Station
Once the busiest in the country, Dunedin Railway station was designed in the Flemish Renaissance style by Railway Department architect George Troup. The recently restored floor of the distinctive ticket hall is a unique mosaic of Royal Doulton.

LINDIS PASS, CENTRAL OTAGO

1 2

The whole landscape had a fresh empty look, almost primeval, almost of the first age of the world.

James Courage

The tussock-clad hills around Lindis Pass offer one of the bleakest prospects in the country, but have a drama all their own. The summit of Lindis Pass (2), at 965 m, is towered over by Doublet Peak (1), 1323 m, and the stark escarpment of Longslip Mountain (3) (1494 m).

The pass was familiar to Ngai Tahu travellers, who would come up the Waitaki River to reach Central Otago long before Otago surveyor John Turnbull Thomson crossed the hills here in 1857. He named the pass after Lindisfarne, or Holy Island, off his native Northumberland, which was the home of the saints and monks who brought Celtic Christianity to England in A.D. 635.

In 1858, a travelling Maori told Canterbury farmer John McLean of uninhabited country over the Lindis Pass. McLean was guided over the pass by chief Te Huruhura and saw vast tracts of tussock-covered land suitable for sheep. He and his brother persuaded the authorities to grant a licence for four runs of 200,000 hectares, with the usual proviso that the land be adequately stocked within one year. This was beyond their means, but a good supply of whisky was not, and this proved to be their salvation. When the government stock inspector arrived to verify that the condition of the lease had been met, he was greeted with true highland hospitality. By plying the inspector with whisky while moving the sheep from block to block, McLean managed to give the appearance of fully stocked runs. His Morven Hills station went on to be a very successful enterprise, with between 135,000 and 250,000 sheep. The stone woolshed, which could house 1500 sheep at a time, still stands.

265°

3

Map ref. [40]

Hills near Lindis Pass
In the glare of the midday sun, the landscape seems featureless, but the evening light brings the hills to life by highlighting the ridges and furrows created by erosion.

Rippon Vineyard, Lake Wanaka

This photograph was taken from the idyllic Rippon vineyard on the shores of Lake Wanaka. Visit the vineyard for a wine tasting, enhanced in the Christmas holidays by gourmet lunches, and savour the view, too.

The shores of Lake Wanaka were used as temporary encampments by Maori for fishing and fowling, but were left deserted after a bloody raid by the Ngati Tama warrior Te Puohi in 1836.

The first European to see the lake was Nathaniel Chalmers, a sheep drover who explored the southern lakes and Central Otago in 1853. Two Maori guides, including chief Reko, accompanied him on this expedition. Having reached Wanaka, Chalmers became too ill with dysentry to continue over the Lindis Pass as Reko wished. His guides, therefore, made a flax raft and took him down the Clutha River, a tumultuous four day journey to the coast.

Central Otago is the fastest-growing wine region in New Zealand, despite being a marginal area for viticulture. The long, hot daylight hours and cool nights of summer allow optimum ripeness and fruit flavours to be reached slowly, as they are in Champagne and Chablis. This climate also encourages acidity, which allows the wines to age well, and the low rainfall in autumn usually allows harvest to be completed without damage to the crop. The poor to moderate soils, typical of so many of the world's great vineyards, limit leaf growth, and hence encourage fruit development. All these factors have helped Rolfe and Lois Mills produce award-winning wines at this beautiful site.

260°

3   4   Map ref. [41]

Lake Wanaka Hillside
The hills surrounding the lake are seen to best advantage when the sun is low in the sky, as their contours are thrown into sharp relief by the shadows.

SHOTOVER RIVER

1

Shotover sounds like an appropriate name for such a turbulent river, racing between the walls of the gorge it has cut through the rock. It is hard to believe that it was actually named after Shotover Park, a property in tranquil Oxfordshire.

In the 1860s, the Shotover was described as 'the richest river in the world'. In November 1862, the first gold strike in the Shotover was made by Thomas Arthur and Harry Redfern, sheepshearers in the employ of William Rees, the pioneer runholder of what is now Queenstown. Rees tried to keep the rumours of gold quiet until shearing was over, but when this was impossible, he paid his men off. With a third man they panned at Arthur's Point, and within two months of their discovery they had gold to the value of £4,000.

There are numerous goldmining relics along the river, reminders of the gold rush when some made their fortunes here, while others lost their lives. The hulks of later gold dredges, some of which cost more than was ever justified by their gains, still rust by the river. One of the best ways to see the upper part of the Shotover River is to take one of the informative tours through Skippers Canyon, which can be combined with a ride on the Skippers Canyon Jet (2).

Jet boats were designed specifically for use on the shallow, rocky rivers of the South Island, and are able to operate in only a few centimetres of water. The man credited with the invention of the jet boat, Sir William Hamilton, would claim rather to have refined an idea that earlier generations had tried with limited success.

After several years of prototyping, Hamilton and his staff produced a sophisticated pump, or jet unit, which draws water through an intake at the bottom of the hull and

2

Map ref. [42]

forces it out at high pressure through a nozzle at the rear. The resulting thrust not only powers the boat but is also used for steering.

In 1864, the Pipeline (1) was built across the river at Wire Rope Creek, to carry water to holding dams for the miners' sluices. It was restored in 1994 to give access on foot across the Shotover, and to provide a site for a 102 m bungy jump. The spectacular Skippers Suspension Bridge, built in 1901, which gives access to the old settlement, is also used for bungy jumping.

Jet Boating on the Shotover
New Zealand leads the world in this exhilarating sport, which has developed into a major tourist activity.

KAWARAU GORGE, CENTRAL OTAGO

1 2

Once a fertility in Vanuatu, bungy jumping now brings an abundance of tourists to Central Otago.

People flock to this point on the Kawarau Gorge, not to see a beautiful old bridge preserved as a monument, but for the adrenalin rush of jumping off the bridge attached to a piece of elastic and dipping into the Kawarau River (1) below before rebounding. For some, the vicarious thrill is enough, and the safety of the viewing platform (2) reassuring.

Bungy jumping was brought to the attention of the world media by A.J. Hackett's audacious jump from the Eiffel Tower in Paris in 1987. He opened the world's first commercial bungy jump site here at the Kawarau Suspension Bridge (4) in 1988.

Early crossings of the Kawarau Gorge were made by jumping a narrow gap across what was otherwise a 'natural bridge'. The first European to use that route was Nathaniel Chalmers, the pioneering run-holder who was guided as far as Lake Wanaka in 1853 by two Maori. The natural bridge was also used by gold miners until more satisfactory crossings, ferries and this suspension bridge, were established. One man, the suspected murderer of a Chinese miner, slipped trying to cross the natural bridge while being pursued in the fog. When his swag was recovered a few weeks later, the purse of stolen gold gave witness to his guilt.

All that now remains of the earlier 'bridge' is a pile of boulders in the river below. The Kawarau Suspension Bridge, which was closed to traffic in 1963, was for 80 years a vital transport link for Central Otago. From the time gold was discovered in

210°

3   4   Map ref. [43]

1862, the Gorge made access to the Wakatipu Goldfield hazardous. At the time of its construction by J. McCormick in 1880, the bridge, designed by H.P. Higginson, was described as 'a model structure in both design and workmanship'.

Bungy Jumping
At 43 m, this is one of the lower bungy jumps that are available: the highest in New Zealand is 300 m from a helicopter.

Lake Wakatipu

1

2

...across the lake to a chaos of peaks and ridges, sliding towards the central vertebrae of the island.

M.H. Holcroft

This is one of the finest views in all New Zealand. What more could anyone want? The scale of the mountains around you can be measured by the clouds half way up their flanks.

Wakatipu means 'the hollow of the giant', referring to the Maori legend about the formation of the lake. The giant Matau seized the daughter of a Maori chief, but as he was running off he was knocked down by a fierce wind, and fell into an exhausted sleep. As he slept, the family of the girl set fire to him. The fire burned into the earth, creating a chasm in the shape of his sleeping form: head at Glenorchy, knees at Queenstown (4), feet at Kingston.

The hole filled up with melt water in the spring, and the lake pulsated with his still beating heart. These pulsations, called sieches, are a feature of this and some other lakes around the world. The lake level can rise and fall as much as 12 cm in five minutes, a phenomenon that may be caused by changes in atmospheric pressure.

The first European to see the lake was probably Nathaniel Chalmers, who explored the southern lakes and Central Otago with two Maori guides in 1853. Another group reached the southern shore of the lake in 1855, setting the area alight by dropping a match. In order to escape the flames the party leapt into the lake and stood neck high in the icy water until the danger was over. They then beat a hasty retreat to the Waikaia Plains.

The Remarkables (1) were given their descriptive name in 1857 by pioneer Otago surveyor, Alexander Garvie. At 2343 m high, they make neighbouring Bayonet Peak (2) look like a small hummock.

260°

3 4 Map ref. [44]

View from the Remarkables Road
Five major rivers feed Lake Wakatipu, but it has only one known outlet, the Kawarau River. More water enters the lake than leaves by the Kawarau, so it must have an undiscovered underground outlet.

Waterfront, Queenstown

1 2

There is so much to do in Queenstown: jet boating, fishing, skiing, tramping, shopping, rafting, eating…the list could go on and on.

Queenstown (1) is situated on Lake Wakatipu, surrounded by a glacier-formed landscape of hills and mountains, including the Remarkables (2). The lake itself is the longest of the South Island lakes, and its bed is 89 m below sea level.

The first European known to have explored this area in detail was Scottish sheep drover Donald Hay, who explored the lake by raft in July 1859. At the end of this 14 day expedition, Hay travelled to Dunedin to apply for a land grant to start a sheep run in the region. On arrival, he found that a prospector had already staked a claim on the land. Hay returned to Australia in disappointment.

The first homestead on Queenstown Bay was built by William Rees, who explored the lake later in 1859 with Nicholas von Tunzelman. Rees' station was overrun with prospectors following the discovery of gold on the banks of the Shotover River on 15 November 1862.

Today, Quuenstown is a hub of tourist activities in the South Island. From here you can participate in any number of hair-raising adventures, including bungy jumping, jet boating, white-water rafting, sky diving, hang gliding, parapenting, and paragliding to name but a few. For the less adventurous there are spectacular ski fields in the winter, and for the positively timid there is a gondola ride 446 m up Bobs Peak, with the reward of panoramic views from the comfort of a mountain-top restaurant.

The twin-screw steamer TSS *Earnslaw* (3) was in use on a regular passenger service when owned by New Zealand Railways, but is now used for lake cruises, a relaxing way to see the magnificent alpine scenery. Walter Peak Sheep Station, which has sheep shearing and sheep dog demonstrations, can be visited by a trip on the *Earnslaw*.

295°

Map ref. [45]

The Remarkables
The Remarkables rise steeply above Lake Wakatipu to a ridge of serrated peaks, including Double Cone, the highest at 2343 m. The dramatically ridged west face of the range was shaped by the same glacier that formed the trough occupied by Lake Wakatipu.

West Arm Power Station, Lake Manapouri

1

The construction of the West Arm Power Station, hewn in the heart of a mountain, was a monumental achievement.

This is the largest hydroelectric power station in New Zealand, and it is unique in that the majority of it is underground. The station was built to power a large aluminium smelting plant at Bluff, and the surplus is fed into the national grid.

The high rainfall of Fiordland makes it an ideal area for a hydro-station. The necessary head of water is usually provided by a river dam, but here a difference in height of 178 m between the intake at Lake Manapouri and the outlet at Deep Cove on Doubtful Sound is employed. Water is sourced from both Lake Manapouri and Lake Te Anau.

The scale of the project was massive. A 2 km road tunnel with a 1 in 10 gradient was built to service the enormous underground powerhouse. The powerhouse — 111 m long, 18 m wide and 39 m high — is a granite walled cavern which contains seven generators. Water flows through the intake structure and plunges down seven vertical penstocks to the turbines (1) which drive the generators. The water is discharged through a 9.5 km tailrace tunnel cut through the Main Divide to Deep Cove. Surveys began in 1959 and construction was completed in 1969.

To service the work, a wharf was built at Deep Cove and a road over Wilmot Pass to the West Arm of Lake Manapouri. This allowed materials and plant to be shipped to Doubtful Sound then trucked over the Main Divide. The 23 km of road, with a gradient of 1 in 5 in places, took two years to build. The largest single load that was

Map ref. [46]

transported along it weighed 290 tons, was carried on a 140 wheel transporter, and required two bulldozers and a grader to both pull and push it.

Lake Manapouri
Lake Manapouri's original name was Moturau — a hundred islands. Its current name means 'sorrowing heart' and is perhaps more apt for such an evocative setting.

Pop's View, Milford

1 2

The Milford Road World Heritage Highway stretches from Te Anau to Milford, passing some of the country's finest views on the way.

The lookout (1) at Pop's View is well positioned to enjoy the Lower Hollyford Valley and its surrounding peaks — Mount Christina (2), 2502 m, Mount Lyttle (3), 1896 m, and, in the distance, the Humboldt Mountains (4).

The road from Te Anau to Milford was not begun until 1929, and only finished in its entirety in 1953, with the completion of the Homer Tunnel. The labour of the pre-war years was provided by the unemployed of the Depression, labouring for the Public Works Department for low wages. Each gang was paid on results, with targets being calculated on the performance of the top gangs. The workers brought their families to live in camps along the routes. Life in the camps was arduous, the weather was wet and cold, and in mid-winter the warming rays of the sun only swung over the mountains to reach the camp for a mere 20 minutes a day.

Two km down the road from here is Marian Corner, where a plaque commemorates Dave Gunn, a Hollyford Valley settler who was drowned while fording the river on horseback in 1955. Gunn is remembered for a heroic 21-hour dash for help after the crash of a small plane at Big Bay in 1936. Gunn was on the West Coast when the plane came down and knew that the nearest telephone was 100 km away at Marian Corner, normally a three day journey. He rowed for 20 km, walked for 26 km, and completed the journey by horse, fording the turbulent Hollyford river many times. Once the news had been relayed to the outside world, a doctor was flown from Invercargill to treat the survivors of the crash.

260°

3   4   Map ref. [47]

The Hollyford River
The first Europeans to see the Hollyford Valley were runholders George Gunn and David McKerrow in 1861, but it was named by explorer Patrick Caples in 1863 after his birthplace in Ireland.

Milford Sound

1   2

Toitu he kainga, whatu ngarongaro he tangata.
The land still remains when the people have disappeared.

Milford Sound, known to the Maori as Piopio-tahi (A Single Thrush) is a synthesis of all the grandeur nature can produce. All around, mountains climb to the heavens — Sheerdown Peak (1) (1878 m), Mount Phillips (2) (1446 m), and the classic profile of Mitre Peak (3) (1683 m). The view of Mitre Peak across Milford Sound is one of the most celebrated views in New Zealand, and rightly so, though rarely has it been photographed this way.

The walls of rock enclosing Milford Sound rise a sheer 1200 m above the sea and plunge hundreds of metres below it. The fiords were formed when the sea engulfed deep glacial troughs after the ice had melted. As with all true fiords, the water is deeper in the inner reaches of the Sound than at its entrance.

Waterfalls, such as Bowen Falls (4), drop down the cliffs from hanging valleys which were formed by subsidiary glaciers of the main iceflow. Beech forests cling to the mountainsides almost miraculously, seemingly despite the laws of gravity, and with little soil to nourish them. When a tree falls it brings a whole avalanche of flora with it, blazing a trail of bare rock down the mountain.

In one version of the Maori legend, the gods were so pleased with Fiordland that when they had finished creating it they sat down to admire their work. Hinenui te Pou, the goddess of life and death, was so angry at this complacency that she created the sandfly to goad them into moving on. Today, it is only the liberal application of insect repellent that prevents the sandfly from having the same effect on modern travellers.

305°

3   4   5   Map ref. [**47**]

Milford had long been a source of greenstone for the Maori when the first Europeans, sealers, began to visit it early in the nineteenth century. The first permanent resident of the area was Donald Sutherland who spent two years exploring the area, living off the land and looking for minerals. He gave his name to Sutherland Falls and Sutherland Sound, and christened the 'City of Milford' when it comprised only two huts. He later set up the John O'Groats Hotel to accommodate travellers and tourists, and wrote disparaging remarks in the visitors' book about departed guests.

Rainy Day in Milford Sound
Milford Sound in the sun is spectacular; in the rain it is hauntingly beautiful, and the waterfalls thunder in the swirling mist.

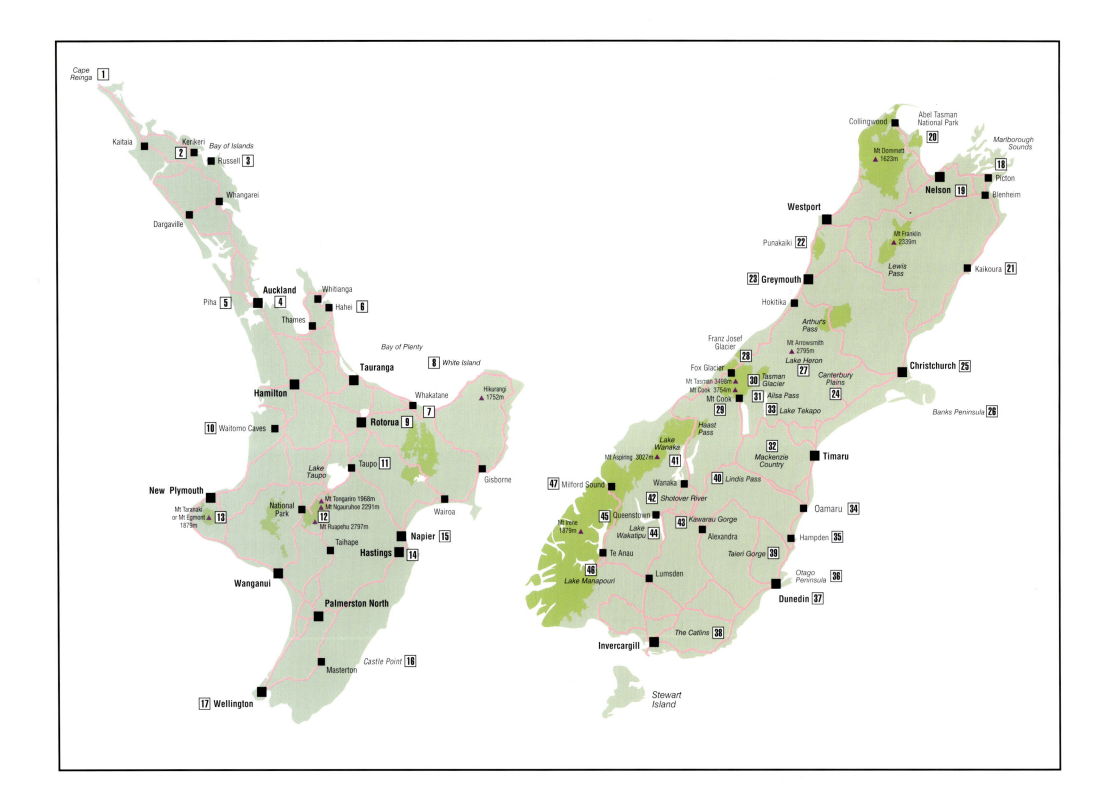